HUDA SHAARAWI was born in Minya, Egypt in 1879 and grew up in Cairo. The daughter of a wealthy and respected provincial administrator from Upper Egypt and a Circassian mother, she was, in the manner of all aristocratic young girls, educated at home. Her memoirs tell of her life as one of the last upper-class Egyptian women in the segregated world of the harem. She was married against her wishes at the age of 13 to a cousin many years older. A year later she separated from her husband for a period of seven years. During these years Huda Shaarawi gradually came to an awareness of the constraints imposed upon women in Egypt and devoted the rest of her life to the fight for women's independence and the feminist cause. With her new-found freedom she took an increasingly militant stand in the harem and became engaged in Egypt's nationalist struggle which culminated in independence in 1922. Her daring act of defiance in unveiling herself at Cairo railway station in 1923 signalled the end of the harem years for herself, and the beginning of the end for others. Until her death in 1947 she was at the head of the Egyptian Feminist Union.

MARGOT BADRAN was born in New York State. Her particular interest in women's lives in the Middle East took her, in the sixties, to Egypt, where she became intrigued by the life and feminism of Huda Shaarawi: she interviewed more than 60 Egyptian women for *Harem Years*. She later took degrees in Middle East Studies at Harvard and Oxford universities, as well as obtaining a Diploma in Arabic from Al Azhar University, Cairo. In the seventies she became increasingly involved in the feminist movement and joined the Institute for Research in History in New York. In 1984 and 1985 she was Jane Watson Irwin Visiting Associate Professor in History and Women's Studies at Hamilton College. She is currently completing a book on the history of the feminist movement in Egypt and divides her time between New York State and Cairo.

Huda as a mature woman.

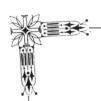

HAREM YEARS

The Memoirs of an Egyptian Feminist
(1879–1924)

by

HUDA SHAARAWI

Translated, edited and introduced by

MARGOT BADRAN

THE FEMINIST PRESS
at The City University of New York
New York

Library of Congress Cataloging-in-Publication Data

Sha'rāwī, Hudá. 1879–1947.
  Harem years.

  Translation of: Mudhakkirātī.
  Bibliography: p.
  1. Sha'rāwī, Hudá, 1879–1947. 2. Feminists—Egypt—
Biography. 3. Women—Egypt—Social conditions. I. Badran,
Margot. II. Title.
HQ1793.S5A3 1987   305.4'2'0924 [B]   86–33620
ISBN 0-935312-71-4
ISBN 0-935312-70-6 (pbk.)

Book designed by Sue Lacey
Cover photograph of Huda Shaarawi courtesy of Hawa Idris
Cover design by Lucinda Geist

Distributed by The Talman Company, Inc., 150 Fifth Avenue, New York,
NY 10011.

CONTENTS

LIST OF PHOTOGRAPHS

All photographs courtesy of Hawa Idris unless otherwise noted.

PREFACE

Towards the end of her life, Huda Shaarawi began to write her memoirs. The decision to record her early, private years was, like much of Huda Shaarawi's life, out of the ordinary. Private life, family life, inner feelings and thoughts were sacrosanct. They were as veiled by convention as women's faces had been. Writing about her life during the harem years was a final unveiling. It can be seen as Huda Shaarawi's final feminist act.

As an upper-class woman, Huda Shaarawi's social language was French. She also knew Turkish, the language of her mother and the Turco-Circassian élites and royal family. But Huda had a special fondness for Arabic, her father's tongue and the national language. In later years, as the feminist movement broadened its base in Egypt and reached out to neighbouring countries, Huda began to use Arabic more and more often in public, especially in her speeches.

It was in Arabic that Huda recorded her memoirs. She dictated them to her secretary Abd al-Hamid Fahmi Mursi. According to Hawa Idris, a younger cousin of Huda Shaarawi and confidante in later years, Huda entrusted her to oversee the publishing of the memoirs if she died before her task was complete. Huda Shaarawi died on 12 August 1947.

Exactly twenty years after Huda Shaarawi's death, while I was in Egypt doing research on the feminist movement and its leader, I met Hawa Idris at a bazaar organized by the Huda Shaarawi Association (formerly the Egyptian Feminist Union) to raise money for the victims of the June War of 1967. I also met Saiza Nabarawi who had first taken off the veil with Huda and had been at her side for the duration of the movement as editor of *L'Egyptienne*, the journal of the Egyptian Feminist Union. The daughter-in-law of Huda Shaarawi,· Munira Asim, for a time president of the Huda Shaarawi Association, was also present along with others who had worked with Huda. It was the beginning for me of a number of associations that grew into lasting friendships.

Hawa Idris immediately invited me to see her at home. I shall never forget visiting her at her apartment in Antikhana Street, not far from the spot where Huda's house with its priceless Islamic treasures had once stood. There in the heart of Cairo Hawa made vivid to me the intense and exhilarating decades of the feminist movement her elder cousin had led. My excitement culminated when Hawa retrieved from a cabinet the notebook containing Huda Shaarawi's memoirs. Only later did I dare ask if I might borrow the memoirs to read them fully. It was a mark of her trust that she handed the notebook to me.

Over the following years, as I came and went from Egypt, Hawa Idris shared long hours with me discussing the life and work of Huda Shaarawi. Meanwhile, I had been searching far and wide, in libraries, archives, and private collections in Egypt and abroad, for other women's accounts of their lives. However, I found nothing like the memoirs of Huda Shaarawi. More and more I realized how rare this document was. I proposed to Hawa Idris that I translate the memoirs of Huda Shaarawi into English and she agreed.

Writing one's own memoirs is a demanding task. Preparing the memoirs of another for publication is more difficult, and more difficult still when they must be translated into another language. Yet Huda Shaarawi's memoirs have long ceased to be a strange, new document to me, although my interest in them remains as fresh as on the day I first saw them. I began translating *Mudhakirrati* (*My Memoirs*), as Huda Shaarawi penned on the cover of her notebook, while I was a student of Arabic at al-Azhar University in Cairo. I used to discuss the subtleties of the meanings of words and passages with my teacher, Shaikh Yahia Hashim. At the same time my historical research helped me to understand the wider context and finer points in the memoirs. But it was the close collaboration – the long hours spent talking together – with Hawa Idris that provided a subtle link with the author of the memoirs and leads me to hope that the English version of the memoirs will echo, as much as possible, Huda's own voice.

A word should be said about the technicalities of presentation. An Introduction provides historical background to the memoirs. I have arranged the account of Huda's private or harem years, hence the title, in four parts with separate headings. In turn, these major parts are divided into smaller sections with their own headings. Some re-ordering of the text was dictated by chronology and by the concern to preserve the natural flow of the narrative. There were also some minor deletions to remove repetitions or the occasional over-elaboration. Another kind of intervention was the removal to an Appendix of material Huda introduced to refute charges of her father's complicity in the entry of the British into Egypt in 1882. This, however important for her to put on record and for the interested historian, does not form part of the central narrative of her own reminiscences.

After Part Four, Huda's account changes in tone and content. She begins to speak about how she and other women became nationalist activists and started the feminist movement. This portion of her memoirs becomes fragmentary. Yet, these 'fragments' are vivid distillations of the extraordinary experiences of herself and other harem women at a moment of tense upheaval and daily uncertainty when some rules were suspended and others adhered to scrupulously. It seemed best to weave this portion of Huda's memoirs into an historical Epilogue.

Everything unless otherwise indicated is from Huda's memoirs. Notes to the text provide further explanation and sources for scholars and the interested general reader. I have put my editorial comments in brackets. I have followed a standard system of transliteration from Arabic into English. However, special signs on letters, the transliteration of the *hamza*, and the transliteration of the *ayn* – except in certain cases when it is rendered as 'a', as in 'Shaarawi' – have been eliminated so as not to clutter the text for the general reader; the specialist will know where they belong. Arabic words which frequently appear in English texts are rendered in their common spelling. An example is the word 'harem', which appears in English dictionaries. The standard transliteration 'harim', would be unfamiliar to the general reader.

This book owes its completion to many people. In Cairo, first thanks are due to Hawa Idris for giving me permission to publish her cousin's memoirs in English and for sharing her memories of growing up in Huda's house and later years as a feminist colleague and confidante to her cousin. I appreciate her continued encouragement and her careful reading of the English text as well as the loan of many priceless photographs. I am grateful to Saiza Nabarawi for sharing stories of her trying adolescence in the Cairo

4

harem world into which she was thrust after a Paris childhood, of the unveiling and feminist movement days with Huda. Meetings with Munira Asim, Huda's daughter-in-law and Bahiga Rashid (both of whom were president of the Huda Shaarawi Association at different times, an association whose library I used), Nini Lanfranchi, Huda's granddaughter; and Mary Cahil, a pioneering philanthropist and feminist, were all illuminating. To Shaikh Yahia Hashim goes my gratitude for long hours teaching me Arabic at al-Azhar University. I thank Prince Hassan Aziz Hassan for lending me a photograph of Khediva Amina from his family collection.

I acknowledge a special debt of gratitude to Albert Hourani who supervised my doctoral thesis at Oxford on Huda Shaarawi and the Egyptian feminist movement and appreciate his valuable comments on the presentation of the memoirs. I thank Afaf Lutfi al-Sayyid Marsot of the University of California at Los Angeles for her helpful remarks on the introduction. For early reactions to her memoirs I am grateful to the Women's Anthropology Group at Oxford and especially to Shirley Ardener and Juliette DeBoulay. Discussions with feminist historians at the Institute for Research in History at New York, in particular Dorothy Helly, Marjorie Lightman and Bill Zeisel provided useful comparative insights. I express appreciation for financial support to the American Research Center in Egypt and to the Warden and Fellows of St Antony's College, Oxford, in the early years of my research. I thank the Department of Near Eastern Studies at Princeton University and especially Carl Brown, for welcoming me as a visiting fellow at the time I was putting the finishing touches to the manuscript. At Hamilton College I thank my colleagues and students for being sources of support and stimulation. To Ursula Owen of Virago goes my appreciation for her enthusiastic response to the manuscript and astute editorial suggestions. I thank Cathy Bellinger, Jane Frost, Laurie Moses and Julie Kisiel for their skills, speed, and good cheer in typing various drafts of the manuscript.

I wish to dedicate my efforts to my husband, Ali Badran who encouraged my exploration of Egyptian life and generously backed me every step of the way; to my father, Joseph Farranto, who has given me his enthusiastic support all my life, and to the memory of my mother, Margaret Woods Farranto, from whom I learned what feminism was before I could put a name to it. She read the memoirs and shared her sharp insights with me.

CHRONOLOGY

1879	Huda Shaarawi born in Minya, Upper Egypt
1881	Brother, Umar Sultan, born
1882	British Occupation of Egypt begins
1884	Father, Sultan Pasha, dies
1888	Memorized the Koran
1891	Betrothed to cousin, Ali Shaarawi
1892	Marriage
1893–1900	Lived apart from husband
1890s	Attended first salon for women led by Eugénie Le Brun
1903	Daughter, Bathna, born
1905	Summer in Turkey. Son, Muhammad, born
1908	Eugénie Le Brun dies. Marguerite Clement inaugurates first 'public' lectures for women
1909	Helps found *Mabarrat* Muhammad Ali
1914	British impose Protectorate on Egypt. Helps found the Intellectual Association of Egyptian Women. First trip to Europe. Mother, Iqbal Hanim, dies
1917	Brother, Umar Sultan, dies
1918	Malak Hifni Nasif, 'Bahithat al-Badiyya', dies
1919	Egyptian Revolution begins. Egyptian Wafd created. The first women's demonstration
1920	Women create the Wafdist Women's Central Committee. Becomes president of WWCC
1922	British rescind Protectorate in unilateral declaration of Egyptian independence. Husband Ali Shaarawi dies. Calls women's boycott meeting
1923	Egyptian constitution promulgated. Electoral law restricts suffrage to males. Founds and becomes president of the Egyptian Feminist Union. Leads EFU delegation to international feminist meeting in Rome. Takes off veil

6

1924	Women picket opening of Parliament. Women present List of Nationalist and Feminist Demands. Resigns as president of the Wafdist Women's Central Committee
1923–47	Leads feminist movement
1945	Decorated by the state
1947	Dies

INTRODUCTION

At Cairo station one spring day in 1923, a crowd of women with
veils and long, black cloaks descended from their horse-drawn
carriages to welcome home two friends returning from an international feminist meeting in Rome. Huda Shaarawi and Saiza
Nabarawi stepped out on to the running board of the train. Suddenly Huda – followed by Saiza, the younger of the two – drew
back the veil from her face. The waiting women broke into loud
applause. Some imitated the act. Contemporary accounts observed how the eunuchs guarding the women frowned with displeasure. This daring act signalled the end of the harem system in
Egypt. At that moment, Huda stood between two halves of her
life – one conducted within the conventions of the harem system
and the one she would lead at the head of a women's movement.

The *Harem Years* of Huda Shaarawi (1879–1947) is an account of
the first portion of her life. It will appeal to anyone eager to know
about life in the harem – a word highly charged in the western
popular imagination. A whole literature grew up in the West in
the nineteenth century – a pot-pourri of travellers' tales and ex-
patriates' accounts that produced a lurid imagery. The harem visit
became *de rigueur* for western women visitors to Egypt, while men
had to content themselves with second- or third-hand reports.
First-hand accounts by women who lived in harems are rare.

The word harem, which to western eyes usually conjures up a
host of exotic images, was simply the portion of the house where
women and children conducted their daily lives. Harem also sig-
nified a man's wife or wives, and it connoted respect. In Egypt, as
elsewhere in the cities of the Middle East, among the upper and
middle classes in the nineteenth and early twentieth century (and
even today in some places) women and men were kept apart.
Women lived their lives within the private enclosures of their
domestic quarters. When they went out they veiled their faces,
thus taking their seclusion with them.

8

The Cairo Railway Station where Huda and Saiza Nabarawi unveiled after returning from the international feminist meeting in Rome in 1923.

Veiling and high seclusion were marks of prestige and sought-after symbols of status. Only the few very wealthy families could afford the most elaborate measures for secluding women – the grand architectural arrangements and eunuchs (castrated men who were usually slaves from Sudan) to guard their women and act as go-betweens with the outer world. In the houses of the poor, women and men were crammed together in the same, limited space. However, when poor women went out – as they did far more often than their richer sisters – they too veiled. Life was different in the countryside, where any visitor could plainly see peasant women moving about freely with faces unencumbered by the veil.

Veiling and the harem system were social conventions connected with economic standing. They had nothing whatsoever to do with Islam. Even those in Egypt who knew better were usually loathe to admit it publicly, however, for honour was at stake. In Egypt, as in other Mediterranean societies, the honour of men and the family rested upon the sexual purity of women. A way to guard purity was by keeping women secluded. In Egypt during the nineteenth and early twentieth centuries, Jewish, Christian and

Houses in an old section of Cairo. The wooden lattice screens on the protruding windows allowed women to look out without being seen. By Huda's time, the wealthy had started to build villas on garden plots nearer the Nile.

Muslim women in the cities all veiled. Lucie Duff Gordon, a perceptive Englishwoman who lived in Egypt in the 1860s, remarked that the Christians she saw in Upper Egypt were more fastidious than the Muslims in veiling.[1]

By the time Huda Shaarawi was born in 1879, Egypt had undergone a transformation begun early in the century when Muhammad Ali (ruler from 1805–49) had rescued the country from its status as a province of the Ottoman Empire and set it up as a semi-autonomous state. To safeguard the new state he built a modern army. He modernized and expanded the health services to keep his troops fit and to increase the then sparse population of Egypt. He began a secular educational system for males which, by the 1870s, was extended to females. (Private, mainly religious, schools had opened for both sexes earlier.) He introduced important changes in agriculture, especially the cultivation of long-staple cotton in the Nile delta. During the American Civil War in the 1860s, when southern supplies of raw cotton to England were interrupted, Egyptian cotton filled the gap, bringing handsome revenues to Egypt. Around the same time railway lines began to be laid out, complementing the expansion of carriageways begun earlier in the century. In 1869, during the rule of Khedive Ismail (1863–72), the Suez Canal was completed with the help of forced labour from the Egyptian countryside. Cairo was given a new look in time to receive Empress Eugénie from France and hundreds of other foreign visitors. A centrepiece, the new Opera House, brought new outlets for entertainment. By the 1880s, not far to the south of the capital, Helwan, known for its sulphur springs, was developed as a winter resort for the wealthy.[2]

During the nineteenth century, there was a continued expansion of Cairo as Egyptians, and also significant numbers of foreigners, moved to the capital. Men like Huda's father, starting out as village notables and rising through the provincial administration, were attracted to the capital as the Turco-Circassian rule drew Egyptians from different parts of the country into the central administration. Meanwhile, sons of families from the growing rural middle class were attracted to Cairo by new educational and professional opportunities which also provided mobility for young urban men. Daughters of wealthy landowners and the rural middle class only went to Cairo if their families moved there or if they married men who lived in the city. Despite the exodus from the country and a growing absenteeism of many rich landlords rural ties were maintained. Links between branches of families were kept alive. Sometimes, Muslim men, if they went to Cairo in their later years, like Huda's father, had households with wives and children both in their place of origin and in the city.

As Egyptian men, like Huda's father, entered into closer professional relationships with the Turco-Circassian ruling class, ties were cemented through marriage and a certain imitation of lifestyle. The ruling class favoured Circassian women, often slaves, as wives and concubines. They were often acquired at a young age and raised in the harems of the élites where they were prepared for their future lives. There was a certain exchange of these slaves among the wealthy households. Huda's mother was raised in the harem of a wealthy relative in Cairo. These women were symbols of status and marriages with them solidified bonds among households. In the second half of the century many marriages and

Egyptian and European women and men walking and visiting on the pavement in front of Shepheard's Hotel in Cairo. Huda remarks how foreigners seated on hotel terraces like this one cheered the women demonstrators during the revolution.

A reception room decorated in a melange of oriental and western styles, a growing practice among the wealthy from the late nineteenth century. This room is in the house of Mustafa Bey Kamil Yaghan.

concubinal alliances were made between wealthy Egyptian men and Circassian women. The children of such unions, like Huda, were heir to two traditions. It was their task to fuse the dual streams of their heritage at a time when life was in rapid change.[3]

There was contact between upper-class Egyptians and the royal family through visits and at receptions. At the same time, there were definite distances maintained. The royal family of Ottoman origins set themselves apart from the Egyptians. In the tradition of *noblesse oblige* the princesses did good works. They endowed educational institutions such as girls' schools and supported the first Egyptian women's philanthropic society early in the twentieth century. However, the princesses essentially remained aloof from social change.

Meanwhile, during the nineteenth century, Egyptians were coming into more frequent contact with foreigners, mainly Europeans. Numerous study missions of young Egyptian men went to Europe (the first study mission of women was not sent abroad until the beginning of the twentieth century) and a steady stream of western technical experts came into Egypt. The wives and daughters of these foreigners were welcomed by women in the harems – some even became tutors and nannies, as Huda's memoirs indicate. It was also not long before women arrived on their own from Europe to act as governesses in the wealthy households or to teach girls from families of more modest means in the newly proliferating private, church-run schools. Marriage between European women and Egyptian men occurred occasionally. Huda's memoirs speak of the marriage of a French woman, Eugénie Le Brun, to an upper-class Egyptian, Husain Rushdi, later a prime minister.

Travel to Europe became a new habit of wealthy Egyptians. By Huda's time, they had grown accustomed to summering in Europe, instead of following the tradition of the royal family and the Turco-Circassian élite of vacationing on the Bosporus. When Egyptians voyaged to Europe, the customary segregation of the sexes broke down and veils were set aside, to be taken up again immediately upon disembarking at Alexandria. Western travellers to Egypt increased as well. Cook's took the first group of tourists up the Nile the year the Suez Canal was opened, just one decade before Huda's birth. (The word tourist itself is said to have been coined in Egypt around that time.)

New technology and material prosperity altered conditions of everyday life in urban Egypt for the wealthy. Huda's generation was the last in Egypt to experience harem life from childhood through mature adulthood. It was a moment of critical transition for these women.

There was an awareness, relatively early in the nineteenth century, of the need to draw women into the mainstream of national development. In 1832, under the auspices of Muhammad Ali, a school was opened to train women to be medical assistants. Initially it had trouble attracting candidates. Four years later, the ruler appointed a Council for Public Education to investigate creating a state school system for girls, but it proved premature. In the 1860s, Khedive Ismail encouraged advisers like Ali Pasha Mubarak and Shaikh Rifai al-Tahtawi to prepare public opinion to support female education, which they did in two books.[4] Shaikh al-Tahtawi reminded people that Islam extolled education for women and men alike. He also argued that the new society, and families themselves, would benefit from the education of girls. When the first state school for girls finally opened in 1873 under the patronage of Ismail's third wife, Tchesme Afit Hanim, it was an important breakthrough. The Siufiyya School, as it was called, served girls from the more progressive families of high state functionaries and white slaves from the royal and aristocratic households. However, it would take some two generations or more before tuition at school became routine for daughters of upper-class families. Meanwhile, they, like Huda, were entrusted to the care of tutors imported into the harems.

Concern for the development of women also emanated from the centre of Muslim learning, al-Azhar University, in the voice of Shaikh Muhammad Abduh, the Islamic modernist who proclaimed the vital role Islam had to play in modern society. He argued that rational inquiry and concern for the welfare of society must guide the application of Islamic teachings. National development was being impeded because Muslims had neglected the true spirit of Islam, he said, and women especially were kept back. They had been deprived of enjoying full advantage of the rights Islam granted them. He advocated the restoration of these rights.[5]

In the 1890s women began to analyse their own condition. Talk about how social custom but not Islam held women back occurred in upper-class harems. Only in places like Huda's memoirs and family papers do we get hints of this, for these discussions had no public outlet. However, simultaneous to this hidden debate, middle-class women began to write about women's rights and responsibilities in the journals they founded as early as 1892. Most of the early writers and founders of journals were of Syrian Christian background and the products of girls' schools that had begun to appear during the nineteenth century; a few of these early writers were Muslims and Jews. The audience for this writing was other women.

During the same period, a few men neither commissioned by the state nor from the religious community, started to analyse the condition of women. In 1894, a young Coptic (indigenous Christian) lawyer, Murqus Fahmi, published a drama called *The Women in the East* attributing Egypt's 'backwardness', to use the term of the day, to the condition of women and the family. He argued that when women in ancient Egypt and early Islam had enjoyed rights civilization flourished. He was equally critical of Copts and Muslims for secluding women and keeping them down. His book was privately printed in a limited edition and, like the women's writings, had a restricted circulation.

Neither the women's writings nor Fahmi's books which expounded views radical in their day attracted the angry protest that greeted the books of a Muslim lawyer and appellate court judge Qasim Amin, who took up a similar theme. In *The Liberation of Women*, published in Cairo in 1899, he told his readers that Islam did not require women to veil and that veiling and seclusion had kept women from enjoying the rights Islam granted them (an echo of Shaikh Muhammad Abduh) (see note 5). This book and *The New Woman*, published the following year, were read with appreciation by Huda and other women in the harems. However, they elicited an impassioned response from men, who produced more than thirty books attacking Amin.

Against this background of change in the nineteenth century is set Huda Shaarawi's childhood and emergence into adulthood which her memoirs recall. The outlines of her life mirrored those of other upper-class girls: education at the hands of tutors in the harem, closely supervised recreation, an early arranged marriage, motherhood, and a gradual expansion of leisurely and instructive pursuits as an adult.

Huda Shaarawi was born Nur al-Huda Sultan in 1879, on the estate of her father, Sultan Pasha, a notable from Upper Egypt, in the town of Minya, an area rich in sugarcane fields and dotted with ancient temples and tombs. Huda's father had acquired immense wealth in land—he left 4400 *faddans* to his heirs—and by the end of his life had risen through the provincial administration to hold the position of president of Egypt's Chamber of Deputies.

Despite a distinguished career, Sultan Pasha had little formal education, not altogether unusual in his day. He spoke exclusively Arabic. His daughter speaks of his deep love for Arabic poetry and recalls the library he amassed. Perhaps it was to her father Huda owed her own special fondness for Arabic. Sultan Pasha's circle of friends included poets, *shaikhs* (religious men), and provincial administrators, as well as statesmen and others of rank. He received men as diverse as Zubair Pasha, the notorious Sudanese slave trader, Ali al-Laithi, poet laureate to Khedive Ismail, and the Coptic Patriarch, Cyril IV. His everyday world was populated by easterners, not by the Europeans coming to Egypt in growing numbers. An exception was a French engineer, Richard, employed in an hydraulic project in Upper Egypt, with whom Sultan Pasha came into contact as a government administrator.

The final years of Huda's father were clouded when his name became associated with the beginning of the British occupation in Egypt in 1822 following the abortive Urabi revolution aiming to give Egyptians greater access to the higher ranks of the army and government administration. By the 1870s public spending and forced borrowing from western banks at extortionate rates had produced the financial disarray which led in the middle of the decade to the dethronement of Khedive Ismail and the arrival of an Anglo-French Commission to regulate the public debt and supervise spending. The outbreak of the Urabi revolution caused alarm among the foreign creditors who feared for the security of their money. This prompted the entry of the British into Egypt to shore up the power of the khedival throne and signalled the beginning of their seventy-four-year occupation of the country. Sultan Pasha's name has been associated with the British entry. Huda refutes this in her memoirs.[6]

In 1884 Sultan Pasha died. Huda spent her childhood, from age five, in a harem bereft of its master. Her early memories were of a melancholy atmosphere – a household presided over by two mourning women. The guardian Sultan Pasha had designated to look after his children when he was gone, Ali Shaarawi, the son of his sister, came only from time to time to look in on the household.

Huda's mother, Iqbal, was a young, fair Circassian of striking beauty when she became the last of Sultan Pasha's several consorts. Girls brought in from the Caucasus and sold on the block to the great families – until slavery was outlawed in 1877 – were symbols of status in the households of the Muslim élites. Although Iqbal came from the Caucasus she was not sold as a slave. As a small child she fled the Caucasus with her mother and siblings during fighting in the Crimea. They went to Stamboul (the part of present-day Istanbul south of Galata Bridge). Later, still a young girl, Iqbal was sent to relatives in Cairo. From her mother, Huda learned Turkish, which she spoke as a child on visits to the khedival palace or as a grown woman when mingling with princesses and members of the Turco-Circassian élite. Iqbal's heritage came alive to her daughter in the tales of carefree mountain life Circassian slaves told during long evenings in the harems.

Huda had a brother, Umar, two years younger. Growing up with him allowed her to note differences in the way boys and girls were regarded and brought up. Boys were favoured. They were given freer rein and were more indulged than girls. However, if a girl had a brother, she might gain advantages and a little more freedom of movement in his company. We see how this happened in Huda's story.

The harem or household where Huda grew up in Cairo was in the then new and fashionable area of Ismailiyya, nearer the Nile than the medieval core of the city. During the 1860s and 1870s, Khedive Ismail made grants of land to men like Sultan Pasha who had the means to build modern houses in fields where sayyal and acacia grew wild. Here the mature Sultan Pasha kept his Cairo harem – Huda's mother and his wife, Hasiba (who figures in the memoirs) and their children. He himself, however, until the end of his life continued to journey between Minya, where his heart remained, and the Egyptian capital. Huda inherited her father's special attachment to his ancestral land.

In these early years Sultan Pasha's widow, whom Huda called *Umm Kabira* (Big Mother), was a key figure in her life. Huda opened her heart to this woman, daring to ask troubling questions about differences between herself and her brother.

Huda tells us about the education she received, alongside her brother, at the hands of private tutors in the harem household. A *shaikh* was brought in to teach Koranic verses and the rudiments of Arabic. It was unusual for a girl to memorize the Koran, as Huda did, and to receive instruction in Turkish and Persian – poetry and calligraphy – for French had become the language of the upper class. European tutors taught French and such subjects as history and literature. They also instructed in painting and piano, which Huda took up, and which were the proper pursuits of an aristocratic young girl.

Around the age of nine or ten, at the onset of puberty, upper- and middle-class girls in Huda's day would begin to wear a veil and cloak when going out of doors. From that time, Huda's childhood companionship with the sons of family friends and neighbours ceased. Huda registers pain over this separation but does not speak of putting on the veil for the first time, a routine event in a girl's life in those days.

The Cairo house of Huda's childhood with its many high-ceilinged rooms, three storeys, and large garden filled with fruit and flowering trees was the scene of many of the events she recalls in her memoirs. Huda continued to live in the house – in her own apartments – after her marriage at thirteen to her elder cousin and legal guardian, Ali Shaarawi, a man already in his forties with a family of his own in Upper Egypt. (It was more usual for a bride to move into the house of her father-in-law.) After just one year of marriage, Huda separated from her husband for a period stretching to seven years. Such a separation – by no means typical of other young women – came when Huda was emerging into full adulthood, a critical and formative time. Meanwhile, an important shift occurred in the relationship between Huda and her brother. Her childhood companion and rival for attention and privileges became an ally and support to her in her adult life. During the time she remained separated from her husband he played a role in helping expand the borders of her daily life.

The original steel girded Qasr al-Nil Bridge over the Nile connecting the city with Jazira where Huda and her brother went on outings as children with Sayyid Agha. The old palace of Khedive Ismail which became the barracks of the British Army is in the background.

Although still very young himself, Umar helped arrange an outing on the Nile where his sister met a woman who was to play a signal role in her development. Huda took an instant liking to Eugénie Le Brun, which the older woman returned. Eugénie held the first salon for women in Egypt, a forum for Huda – the youngest to attend – and other women to examine their lives and raise questions. The women had been doing this for some time, as noted, when the publication of Qasim Amin's books further stimulated their efforts.

The 1890s were an important juncture in Egyptian history. By that time new possibilities had opened up for expanded learning, mobility, and recreation for the upper classes. Yet notwithstanding intellectual debate, pressures remained to observe the old social rules which for upper-class women meant continuing to lead circumspect, still highly secluded, lives. Men of this class were freer to experiment although they too were held down by inherited imperatives more than most realized. Huda shares with the reader salient experiences of this time.

At the turn of the century when Huda was twenty-one years old, she resumed married life with her husband and within five years had become the mother of a girl and a boy. After a few years focused on domestic concerns she entered another stage in feminist evolution. Huda writes about her role in pioneering the first 'public lectures' (outside private houses but in halls for women only) for women, which carried the discussion begun in the women's salon a step further and widened the circle. Through these lectures upper-class harem women and their middle-class sisters, graduates of the new school for girls, first came together. Here Huda met Malak Hifni Nasif, a graduate of the Saniyya School (formerly the Siufiyya School, mentioned earlier) and daughter of Hifni Nasif who had been a student of the reforming Shaikh Muhammad Abduh at al-Azhar University. Under the pseudonym Bahithat al-Badiyya (Seeker in the Desert), Malak wrote on the condition of women and composed verse. An accomplished speaker, she was the first woman to make public demands for women's rights, in 1911 at the Egyptian Congress in Heliopolis. Huda tells how she herself took the podium for the first time in her life to pay homage to Bahithat al-Badiyya when she died prematurely in 1918.[7]

Another important breakthrough occurred when Huda, with

backing from princesses of the royal family, helped establish the first women's philanthropic society, the *Mabarrat* Muhammad Ali, to run a dispensary for poor women and children. In assisting their most needy sisters the women of the privileged élite also helped themselves. They acquired their first meeting place outside the harem and gained valuable experience in organizing operations and rallying support through fund-raising.

Huda's memoirs culminate in a moment of transition – simultaneously the rise of the Egyptian nationalist movement in which women were active and the decline of the institution of the harem. In an intimate way, Huda was linked to the beginning, and the move to end the British occupation in Egypt. It has already been noted that her father, Sultan Pasha, was implicated in events surrounding the arrival of the British into Egypt and that blame was heaped on him from certain quarters, causing both him and his daughter great bitterness. Huda's husband and the nephew of her father, Ali Pasha Shaarawi, was one of three Egyptian representatives who went to the British High Commissioner in 1918 requesting that an Egyptian delegation go to London to present demands for independence to the British government. When this was denied the men created a party called the Wafd (delegation) to speak for the nation.[8] Ali Shaarawi became the treasurer. Ten months later the Wafdist Women's Central Committee was formed and Huda Shaarawi became the president. It was the Wafdist women and men who led the fight for national independence. The story of the struggle of Huda and other women for national liberation and the transition from the feminism of the harem to a public feminist movement is told in the Epilogue.

The *Memoirs* of Huda Shaarawi have dual significance. They give insight into harem experience in Egypt in its final decades. At the same time they reveal how the roots of upper-class women's feminism in Egypt are found in the nexus of their harem experience and growing change around the turn of the century. We see that women's participation in the national movement did not produce feminism (as frequently assumed) but was the turning point for moving from changes in consciousness and the using of close and expanding connections between women to public activism.

The *Memoirs* provide valuable clues as to why Huda was the first to emerge publicly as a militant feminist. She came from a

Huda with teenage Saiza Nabarawi at her knee in the French salon of her Cairo house.

class able and eager to exploit the advantages of modernization in everyday life, hence supporting innovation, yet a class also eager to maintain its privileges and apartness. Controlling women was seen as crucial to this. Maintaining *visible* honour was dependent upon the seclusion of women and honour had important political implications. Female seclusion separated women from men but also distanced women from different classes. Early Egyptian feminism not only challenged the patriarchal order but was an ideology that superseded class and was all the more threatening to the old order because it was grounded in Islam.

At the level of everyday existence, the old harem life had become untenable for women like Huda. The growing strains and contradictions were becoming insupportable. In Huda's life a particular confluence of larger events and personal circumstances coupled with an acute sensitivity explain her evolving feminism. Huda observed gender inequalities as a young child and suffered from them. Outside circumstances temporarily removed her from marriage, giving her time on her own, when her understanding of what it was to be a woman deepened. She engaged in innovative activities that broke through the narrowness of mainly family circles and, together with other women, created new institutions. When the national independence movement took to the streets she was ready to play an active role and also capitalized on her husband's role as a leading figure in the nationalist movement. However, when independence was announced and the call went out for 'normalization', for women to return to their old harem lives, Huda was free from the controls of a patriarchal family – husband, father and brother were gone. She was a mature woman in her forties. She was ideologically and practically prepared. She had control over vast personal wealth. She had the respect conferred by family and class, sustained by her own irreproachable behaviour, and enhanced by her important role in the independence struggle. Perhaps most important of all, she had courage and commitment. Huda Shaarawi's memoirs are a unique testament to all this.

PART ONE

THE FAMILY

CIRCASSIAN RELATIVES

We used to wait eagerly for the visits of my maternal grandmother and uncles, who came every year or two from Turkey. They would come loaded down with enormous quantities of rare treats, such as spicy salted beef called *basturma*, sausages, Circassian cheese, walnuts, chestnuts, and dried fruits, which we shared with our friends and neighbours.

My grandmother was short and neither fat nor thin, with blue eyes and very pale skin. She dressed all in white and covered her two plaits of white hair, nearly as long as she was, with a gauze *tarha*. In this incandescent whiteness she had the appearance of a saint, and the kindliness that filled her face gave it a special radiance. I loved my grandmother very much even though we did not share a common tongue and I could not communicate with her except in signs. She used to amuse me with Circassian tales and songs, many of which I remember to this day. Yusif, my elder uncle, resembled my grandmother in stature, kind expression, and gentle disposition, and was much cherished by us for his light-heartedness. My uncle, Idris, the father of Hawa and Huriyya,[1] with his slender figure and beautiful face, looked more like my mother. He was a tall, graceful man of exquisite manners who lavished great love and attention upon us and spent long days in conversation with us.

Our relatives used to spend the winter with us, but with the approach of summer my grandmother would begin to show signs of suffering from the heat. Her eyes would swell, her face would flush, and she would insist on returning to Turkey. The separation always pained us.

One year, after his mother and older brother had departed, Uncle Idris remained behind to study Arabic and deepen his knowledge of Islam. My mother urged him to take a wife. When he expressed an interest in marrying an Egyptian girl and my mother arranged his betrothal to the daughter of a respected family, we all rejoiced. The date for the wedding had already been fixed, when the parents of the prospective wife made it a condition for marriage that their daughter never be required to live abroad. Uncle Idris would not agree, insisting that a wife should follow her husband wherever he might go, and thus the engagement was broken.

Years later, after my grandmother had died, Uncle Yusif married and brought his wife to Egypt for a visit. One day, I pleaded, 'Why don't you stay with us instead of returning to Istanbul where there is nothing to keep you after Grandmother's death?' With a smile he said, 'Your father, upon him be blessings, asked me to stay the first time we came to Egypt. I did not agree, because it would have meant the disappearance of the family name in our country.' I pressed him, 'Is Bandirma (a port town on the Sea of Marmara) the home of your father and grandfather? Was the house you now occupy built by your father? You are from the Caucasus not Anatolia, aren't you?' He smiled again and said, 'These were the very words your late father used when he urged me to settle in Egypt.'

Uncle Idris returned to settle in Turkey, where he also married. One day my two uncles and other relatives in Turkey were invited to a wedding celebration in a neighbouring village. In those parts, it was customary on such occasions to travel in ox-drawn carriages because the horses could not pull loads over the rough terrain. When my elder uncle was about to set out for the wedding he asked his brother Idris to accompany him. Since my younger uncle had guests, and could not leave immediately, he promised to follow later on his new mare. When he set out galloping, his high-spirited horse let loose and began to run away with him. The horse reared up unexpectedly. He was thrown to the ground and killed instantly.

News of this turned the rejoicing of the wedding party into mourning. He left behind two little daughters, Hawa and Hurriyya, the elder not yet two and the younger still being suckled.

MY MOTHER

My mother was a strong woman, a private person who had firm control over her emotions. She seldom complained and kept her sadnesses hidden inside. I never once dared ask my mother about her origins and how she came to Egypt. But, very eager to learn about my mother's early life, I urged Uncle Yusif to tell me why his family had left the Caucasus and gone to Anatolia, how my mother had come to Egypt, and about her marriage to my father.

He told me that my mother's father, Sharaluqa Gwatish, had been the renowned headman of the Shabsigh tribe. When fighting broke out between the Caucasus and Czarist Russia in the 1860s, the Circassians defended the Caucasus with singular bravery. However, my grandfather's men were overcome and he was captured. Another tribal leader in the Caucasus, the well-known Shaikh Shamil al-Daghistani,[2] an adversary of my grandfather, discredited him by circulating the story that my grandfather had betrayed his country and joined the Russians. A rival band of Circassians then seized his son Yusif, less than sixteen years old, and held him hostage under pain of execution if the allegations proved to be true. Relatives and friends of my grandfather, meanwhile, set out to rescue him from Russian captivity and save his poor, innocent son. Disguised as Russian soldiers, the Circassian rescue party which included Huriyya, the beautiful and courageous daughter of my grandfather's brother, penetrated enemy ranks. The Russians unfortunately discovered the rescue attempt and killed or wounded most of the Circassians, who were few in number and badly equipped. Despite injuries, my grandfather continued firing at the Russians from behind the mountain rocks, while Huriyya went for help. My grandfather fought until a bullet finally killed him. The Circassian reinforcements carried his body to his birthplace for burial, thus giving lie to the slander spread by his rival, Shaikh Shamil. His son Yusif was thus spared dishonour and death.

Afterwards, my grandmother decided to leave the Caucasus.

With her five young children, three boys and two girls, she joined the stream of refugees making their way to Istanbul. My uncle told me about their suffering from hunger and other bitter experiences. While the Turkish government was still processing the refugees, Jacob, the youngest boy, died from pneumonia as a result of over-exposure. When his little sister was abducted from the woman who suckled her, my grandmother decided to send her other daughter – my mother – to Egypt to be raised under the care of her maternal uncle, Yusif Pasha Sabri, an army officer.

My grandmother entrusted my mother to a friend leaving for Egypt on a visit to Raghib Bey and his family. The man was asked to take my mother to Yusif Pasha Sabri in Cairo. When they arrived, my mother's uncle was on a military expedition abroad, and his wife (a freed slave of il-Hami Pasha[3]), a peculiar woman, protested her husband had no such relative and refused to accept my mother. The man then took my mother to Raghib Bey's house to await her uncle's return. It seems that her uncle's wife remained silent.

My mother stayed where she was. Raghib Bey's daughter cared for her like a daughter and took her with her when she married and set up a new household.

My mother grew into a striking beauty. Her guardian decided to marry her to a wealthy man. It was her good fortune that my father took her as his wife. One day, after she was married, she was standing near the window helping my father dress, when she began to cry. When my father asked her what was the matter, she told him she had seen a young man who looked like her brother enter the *salamlik* (men's reception area). My father asked about her family and she told him her story. He then sent for Ali Bey Raghib to seek their whereabouts. My father located the man who had originally brought my mother to Egypt and dispatched him to Turkey to bring the brothers back.[4]

When my mother's two maternal uncles arrived our clan expanded. The reunion changed my mother's life.

MY FATHER

My father died when I was five years old. I have only a few memories of him, as he was often away from Cairo. I used to go to his room with Ismail, my brother from another wife, to kiss his hand every morning. We would find him sitting on his prayer rug praying or meditating. After we kissed his hand and he kissed us, he would go to his cabinet to get chocolates for us. We always left his presence beaming with joy.

My father played an important role in the political life of Egypt and rendered noble services during his long public career.[5] Unfortunately, I was unable to lay my hands upon historical records to document the story. When I looked for contemporaries of my father, the only person I found who could assist me was Qallini Pasha Fahmi,[6] who as a young man had been closely associated with my father during the last years of his life.

My father entered government service after receiving a letter that designated him Commissioner of the District of Qulusna in the province of Minya. He immediately went to the governor of the province to explain that he could not accept the appointment because he was acting as guardian to his brother, Ibrahim, and the children of his paternal uncle who were still young and needed his care. After much discussion, the governor confided, 'It was your friend Hasan al-Sharii[7] who advised me to appoint you.' My father retorted, 'Why didn't he suggest one of his cousins for the job?' The governor held firm, however, and Father accepted the appointment.

Around that time, the ruler of Egypt, Said Pasha (1854–63) paid a visit to the province of Minya. When he told the governor, Mustafa Bey, that he wished to visit one of the notables of the province, Mustafa Bey suggested either my father or al-Sharii Pasha. Because Father's village was closer, the ruler decided to visit him first. While he sat with Father in the *kiosk* in the garden, he asked, 'Why don't you build a house worthy of yourself? Do you think I am like Abbas Pasha (ruler of Egypt 1848–54) who did not wish to see symbols of wealth in his subjects? I wish all my subjects to have mansions and palaces like my own.' In reply my father said, 'We understand the wishes of him who has given us prosperity, and we beseech God that he will live long and will honour us with his presence in mansions worthy to receive him.'

Said Pasha replied, 'God willing.' Later, when Father was deputy governor of Bani Swaif and he heard of Said Pasha's imminent visit to Upper Egypt, he put the finishing touches on his new house and garden.[8] There he spent hours poring over *Mustatraf fi Kull Mustazraf* and other books.[9] Some people gossiped that he was taken up by books and had no time for the demands of administration.

However, Father went on to become governor of Bani Swaif, then Asyut, and finally Rudah al-Bahrain. He also served as deputy inspector of Upper Egypt and went on to become Inspector General.

During that time a rift developed between him and Khedive Ismail (1863–79) who had succeeded Said Pasha as ruler of Egypt. One day when the khedive was touring Minya he asked Father if Abu Hamadi would make a good governor of Minya. (The governor at the time was Aslan Pasha.) Father demurred. The khedive repeated his question, and Father finally responded, 'He would be good as governor of Suhag, his own province. Is not the present governor of Minya competent?' He added, 'Afandinah, it is better to assist Minya instead of being concerned with changing the governor.'

On the train to Cairo, a few days later, the khedive asked Father about tax collection. 'Your majesty,' my father said, 'has sought my opinion twice before and I have given it, and now you ask about tax collection. It would be more beneficial to the public welfare if His Majesty were to concern himself with improving the condition of his subjects.' The khedive became enraged at such outspokenness and ordered Father to leave the train immediately, even though it was in motion. Father was preparing to jump off when, by God's will, the train stopped, perhaps to fill up with water, and the khedive suddenly relented.

Following the incident on the train, the khedive appointed my father head of the Legal Consultative Council at Khartoum, in the Sudan, a posting that amounted to exile. Father lost the use of the train, *Tair Khair* (Good Omen), that had been placed at his disposal for inspection trips in his province. Friends of my father began petitioning important personages on his behalf. Nubar Pasha, Sharif Pasha, and Riyad Pasha[10] went to the khedive pleading that the country needed Father's services. Other friends petitioned the khedive's mother. His devotion to her was widely known. Finally, Ismail Pasha Saddiq,[11] Ahmad Khairi Pasha, and Shaikh Ali al-Laithi went to Prince Taufiq (he became ruler of Egypt in 1879). It seems his intervention was the reason the khedive rescinded the order.

Father had already set out for the Sudan and had reached Rudah (a Cairo port for Nile traffic to the South), when word came that the order had been lifted. After his return from Rudah the khedive's mother gave him a golden *zarf* encrusted with diamonds and emeralds and other gifts I cannot recall now.

My father had been maligned by certain so-called patriots, distorters of history, who have recently charged that he assisted the entry of the British into Egypt by bowing to the wishes of Khedive Taufiq (1879–92).*

Two severe shocks ruined my father's health. One was the death of my brother, Ismail, upon whom Father had placed all his hopes. The boy was possessed of intelligence and lively curiosity. In every respect, he seemed older than his age. He was not yet four when he died. My other brother, Umar, less than two at the time, was not of good health and hopes for him were slim. The second shock was the Urabi tragedy.

My father died on 14 August 1884 in Graz. He had gone abroad to consult eminent physicians in Austria and Switzerland when doctors in Egypt had been unable to cure him.

---

* *This refers to events surrounding the revolution led by the Egyptian army officer, Ahmad Urabi, in 1881 and 1882. Sultan Pasha at first supported Urabi and his followers who sought greater access for Egyptians to the higher ranks of the army, until then mainly the preserve of the Turco-Circassians. This was part of the bid to increase the participation of Egyptians in running their country. However, Sultan Pasha became disenchanted with Urabi and withdrew his backing. He feared the British would intervene as they were interested in safeguarding the rule of the khedive to keep lines to India open. The Urabi revolution failed and the British occupied Egypt. Some said that Sultan Pasha facilitated their arrival when he threw his support to the khedive. Years later when his daughter – who was only three when the British set foot in Egypt – heard stories from those days she was deeply saddened. His daughter tells how these events and recriminations cast a shadow on his last days. She held the vision of her father as a fervent Egyptian patriot who had pioneered in the development of his country. Before her own death, she wished to clear her father's name. She took the opportunity of her memoirs to make her case. This appears in full in the Appendix.*

Sultan Pasha, Father of Huda.   *Chalk drawing of Iqbal Hanim, Mother of Huda.*

I sent for Shaikh Abd al-Rahman Qaraa, who had accompanied a companion of my father, to learn about his final voyage. He gave me the following document.

On the eve of our departure from Alexandria Hasan Pasha Abd al-Raziq, Muhammad Uthman Bey al-Hilali, and Ali Bey Shaarawi were present. I believe Hijazi Bey and al-Sayyid Ibrahim al-Sanusi were there, as well. Sultan Pasha recited a few lines of his poems to us. One began:

> I think of Egypt, defending her children and
>   caring for them.
> I hold back all who trammel her rights though
>   banners fly o'er their heads.

Sultan Pasha gave me a piece of paper upon which he had written a eulogy of his son, Ismail. I can still recall the following:

In my grief and distress let me
   endure what I must.
Let me weep alone,
   no one can mend my heart's wounds.
Avenging fate has struck a blow
   that can level mountains.
It wrested my soul's companion,
   my joy and my life.
I guarded him for the glory to come after me,
   that he might build on a strong foundation.
But time hastened to him before me;
   my hopes lay crumbled.
Oh, God, you are my God,
   cast me not aside
   without solace or succour.

I knew Sultan Pasha was suffering from a kidney disease and that it was growing worse. When he decided to seek a cure abroad he was growing worse. When he decided to seek a cure abroad he asked Shaikh Ali al-Laithi to accompany him. He agreed to accompany him to Lebanon but if he wished to go to Europe, he suggested that I should travel with him. When Sultan Pasha asked me to accompany him to Europe, I happily agreed.

While we were in Graz, Khedive Ismail (then in exile) was in the same hotel. When the ex-khedive learned of Sultan Pasha's arrival he made known his wish to call upon him and indeed did so a week before his death.

After some time in Graz, we departed, only to retrace our steps later. The evening of our return to Graz, Sultan Pasha requested me to remain in his room, which I did. In the morning he summoned his servant, Ali, to bring him his ewer and basin so he could wash. Meanwhile I left to make my ablutions and morning prayer. I was in my room when Ali hastened saying, 'Come quickly!' I rushed to the Pasha's room and found him with his eyes wide open. With Ali's help I carried him to his bed and immediately sent for Qallini Fahmi Pasha and Musa Shukri, who were also in the Pasha's party. They called for the doctor, who came and pronounced him dead.

Qallini Pasha wired Nubar Pasha, then the Prime Minister of Egypt, and he wired Blum Pasha, the Egyptian Minister of Finance, who was in Vienna at the time, to take care of the necessary expenditures since Sultan Pasha's money was held up in bonds. The body was embalmed and returned to Egypt.

In 1924, when I attended a conference on ethics in Graz, I did not know my father had died there. We knew only that he had left Graz for Switzerland and understood he had died there. When I returned from the conference, Qallini Fahmi Pasha asked me where I had stayed, and when I told him the Elephant Hotel, he said, 'Your father died in that hotel. After the doctors in Switzerland gave up hope to cure him they advised him to return home. Feeling tired and weak on the return journey he decided to stop in Graz. He stayed only one night. The following morning he died.'

The next year I returned to Graz and stayed in the same hotel. I summoned the director to inquire if the registers for 1884 were still available. He replied no, asking the reason for my request. I told him my father had died that year in this hotel and I wished to see the room where his spirit left him. He expressed his regret for the lack of records for that period, explaining they had been discarded when the hotel was renovated. He paused a moment, bowing his head in silence, and promised to look into the matter.

That evening he came to my room with a doctor who had been present at my father's death. I was surprised to see how young he was. He explained that he was a medical student at the time and had accompanied one of the doctors. He told me my father had been found dead. He added he was certain an official report was made following the autopsy and promised to check the records at the Municipality. Two days later he presented me with a copy of the official report.

The doctor told me that the government of Austria had honoured my father with a large ceremony and that the government of Egypt had sent an official who was summering in Austria to take part in rendering homage. How grief-stricken I was that night in the hotel, shrouded in painful memories!

PART TWO

CHILDHOOD IN THE HAREM

1884–92

TWO MOTHERS

During that long, grim night in Graz, I recalled the day they announced the death of my father – the days of grief and the long, gloomy years to follow when the furniture was draped in black. I saw my mother, lying distraught in bed with doctors calling on her from time to time, and my brother and me being brought to her bedside. Gazing on us with tearful eyes she would bury her head under the covers pleading, 'Take the children away.' The spectre of my mother, not yet twenty-five when my father died, loomed with intense clarity, mingling with other scenes from my childhood.

I recalled going to see *Umm Kabira* (Big Mother),[1] the mother of our deceased brother, Ismail. She occupied a room next to our mother's. There we would witness the still more harrowing sight of a young woman who had recently lost her son now grieving also at the death of her husband. Abandoning all hope in life, she had fallen ill and clung to her bed the eight years that remained to her. Occasionally, when she yielded to pleas to take a little exercise and walked from room to room, my brother and I ran ahead of her clapping with excitement. I remember during those rare moments her face lighting up with a sweet smile tinged with sadness, whose memory pains me to this day. Despite suffering and spending her final years in bed, she learned to read the Koran

34

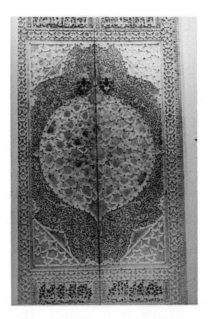

Elaborately worked wood and metal door of Huda's house in Cairo.

with the help of a teacher who gave her daily instruction. This brought her a little solace.

I loved *Umm Kabira* immensely, and she returned that love and showed compassion toward me. She, alone, talked frankly with me on a number of matters, making it easy for me to confide in her. She knew how I felt when people favoured my brother over me because he was a boy. She, too, occasionally fanned the flames of jealousy in me, but without diminishing my love for my brother.[2]

The affection my mother showed me often intensified my agonies because her solicitude, I fancied, was merely an effort to cajole me. If my mother saw me growing jealous while she played with my brother she would hasten with him to my side. At such a moment, I feared I was coming between them, and my anguish would redouble. Yet, it was, indeed, kindness and love that inspired her.

I used to imagine that I was not my mother's daughter — that my real mother was a slave girl who had died, and the truth was being withheld from me. Firmly convinced of this, I suffered all the more. I could keep everything suppressed until nightfall but as soon as I laid my head on the pillow, I was overcome by anxieties and frightening thoughts moved me to tears. This inner turbulence provoked nightmares that woke me in terror, with heart beating so hard I feared it would escape from my chest. I dreamed often that huge beasts were pouncing on me, baring their fangs in my face, and that when I sought refuge with my mother I would find that she had taken my brother in her arms and turned her back on me. 'I am not your child!' I would scream, 'You have lied to me! Tell me the truth! I am not your child! I am not your child!'

Childhood perplexities and self-inflicted torments increased my need for warm affection and swelled my love for the father I had barely known. If he were still alive, I knew, he would not withhold his comfort. My anguish was lessened a little by my belief that the dead see us even though we cannot see them and that contact between their spirits and ours enables them to feel what we feel. Thus I strove to improve myself so that the spirit of my father would be content and remain with me always. In my dark moods I retrieved my father's picture from its secret hiding place and held it close to me, telling it my woes and believing it heard me. The face seemed to grow sad, the eyes gazed upon me with profound compassion, and immediately my soul grew quiet.

In these states of agitation I sometimes confessed my sufferings to *Umm Kabira* and she consoled me. Often, my mother granted permission to spend a few nights with *Umm Kabira*, paying no heed to her respiratory ailment because the notion of contagion never troubled my mother. I thus spent nights sleeping peacefully in the same bed with *Umm Kabira*, talking with her until sleep overtook me. Unlike my mother, who insisted upon closing the windows and doors for fear the fresh air would make us ill, *Umm Kabira*, like me, could not sleep unless the windows were open, especially in summer. After sleeping in *Umm Kabira*'s room, I would awake, invigorated, in the early hours of the morning to the sounds of chirping birds and the gardener unlatching the gates. Feeling deep joy in communion with nature, my spirit would soar to the heavens. Later *Umm Kabira* and I would take breakfast together. We usually had *qishda* (clotted cream made by boiling the rich milk of the water buffalo) which we spread on bread and fresh fruits.

There were other happy moments, like the winter evenings we

sat warming ourselves by the coal brazier. I would place chestnuts on the glowing embers and wait for them to crack, as *Umm Kabira* looked on tenderly.

I once asked *Umm Kabira* why everyone paid more attention to my brother than to me. 'Haven't you understood yet?' she asked gently. When I claimed that as the elder I should receive more attention she replied, 'But you are a girl and he is a boy. And you are not the only girl, while he is the only boy. One day the support of the family will fall upon him. When you marry you will leave the house and honour your husband's name but he will perpetuate the name of his father and take over his house.' This straightforward answer satisfied me. I began to love my brother all the more because he would occupy the place of my father.

Soon, however, my uneasiness returned. I repeated my question once again, this time to my mother, who said, 'Your brother has a weak constitution and, as he is the only boy, naturally, everyone is solicitous of him. You are in good health and so people do not have the same concern over you.' Although her words restored my tranquillity, I was also saddened because I saw that my anxieties upset her.

I then hoped to become sick in order to claim equal attention from her. It happened that an illness was circulating and so I was delighted to be the first in the house to come down with it. Unaccustomed to see me ailing, my mother grew concerned and immediately called the family doctor, Alwi Pasha.[3] At the end of the examination, I remember, he took out a piece of white paper, shaped it into a cone and poured alum powder into it which he blew into my throat. He also prescribed a mineral purgative. That whole night my head burned with fever.

A few days later, when my brother fell ill, the entire household was plunged into turmoil. Doctors entered our room in groups. One by one they examined my brother, afterwards leaving without so much as a glance at me even though my bed was next to his. That upset me profoundly. Until then I had been responding to the treatment but I suddenly began to take a turn for the worse. Although I was seized by fits of trembling which caused the fever to rise, no one appeared concerned. When my condition continued to grow worse, Alwi Pasha was sent for a second time but did not arrive until a day later, when he appeared in the company of the doctors returning to visit my brother. He stayed with them while they examined my brother, conferring about his further treatment, only looking at me as he made his way to the door. I nearly fainted from distress. My convalescence persisted until my brother was out of bed. I began to prefer death to my miserable lot.

After that I withdrew into myself and resented those around me. I began to spend the afternoons in the garden amid the fruit and flower trees, and the birds, fish, and pet animals. I preferred the companionship of these creatures to the company of humans who injured my self-esteem. I grew attached to a gazelle that followed me everywhere. It would climb to our room on the top floor, come over to my bed, and put its head on my pillow to rouse me with its sweet whine before proceeding to my brother's bed. If I was sick, however, it would remain loyally at my side like a cat or dog. This affection consoled me very much. I loved animals and believed they instinctively sensed my condition.

MY BROTHER

Despite my jealousy I loved my brother very much. My attachment to him was strengthened still more by an incident that occurred one day while we were playing alone on the upstairs balcony. We were going to visit the children of Thabit Pasha later that afternoon. Since their father wished to see us I told my brother we would have to change our clothes. He turned to me with a soulful look in his eyes and asked, 'Why don't we have a father like theirs? Whenever I ask *dada* (nanny) about him she says he is away on a long journey but I wonder why he never returns.' I asked, 'Don't you know the reason?' He replied, 'No, can you tell me?' 'Yes,' I answered, 'but you must promise to keep it a secret.' When he gave me his promise I said, 'They are lying.' With a look of amazement he asked me why. I told him, 'Because our father is dead.'

Immediately I regretted my words, for he threw himself on the floor kicking and shrieking hysterically. Horrified, I tried to soothe him but to no avail. My mother rushed in and asked what was wrong. I disappeared behind the door fearing that if he repeated what I had said my mother would vent her anger on me. I remained hidden for some time, trembling in fear. My mother lifted my brother off the floor and held him close to her, drying his

Huda and her brother Umar.

tears and trying to comfort him, but he continued to cry and was unable to speak. She asked me sharply, 'Did you strike your brother?' He murmured, gasping for breath, 'No, *Alba* (big sister) didn't do anything to me.' She thought an insect might have bitten him but could find no marks. His agitation persisted for some time before he fell asleep in her arms. We were concerned that the outburst would injure his health. He did not leave his bed for the next two days. My mother tried to extract the cause of his tantrum from each of us but my brother never breathed a word. Rather than invent a story to appease her, he remained true to his word, a habit that stayed with him for life, but he never again asked where his father was, because he knew. Since that day my love for my brother deepened and his tenderness towards me grew. We shared the same room, the same lessons, and the same play.

THE EUNUCHS AND THE MAID

Bashir Agha, the oldest of my late father's eunuchs,[4] a merry man with a deep laugh, was an awesome and venerable personage, held in high esteem by friends of the family and all others who knew him, but not so much by my brother and me, as he used to take us to task. He had numerous friends of all ranks and classes. His light-heartedness and praiseworthy virtues earned the nickname 'Abu al-Bashir', Father of Mankind. An inveterate better on horse races and ram and cock fights (he owned a number of animals himself), he tried to interest my brother, of whom he was very fond, in these pursuits. I feared it would distract from his lessons, but my mother's maid, Fatanat, entrusted to look after my brother when his Sudanese nursemaid died, tried to persuade him he had no need for learning because he was rich. I threatened never to speak to him again if he didn't pay attention to his studies.

Said Agha, a younger and more severe man, was charged to watch over us and all who came to the house. He accompanied us everywhere and was even present during our lessons. The household staff feared him because he observed every minute detail. He was 'master of life and death' over the servants and tutors.

My mother's maid, Fatanat, a source of intrigue and conflict, took a dislike to me. A Frenchwoman, Mme Richard, used to pass many hours with me, and the maid would carry tales about her to my mother in order to create difficulties. She also made trouble with the two young girls, one an Egyptian and the other a Circassian, who were raised with us as our companions. She even tried to sow discord between my mother and myself but to no avail.

LESSONS AND LEARNING

My brothers and I and our two companions began our daily lessons early in the morning and finished at noon. We took up various subjects with tutors who came to the house under the supervision of Said Agha. I was devoted to my studies and became completely absorbed at lesson time.[5]

Of all the subjects, Arabic was my favourite. One day when I asked the teacher why I was unable to read the Koran without

Eunuch with young charges (girl to the far right, little niece in the Memoirs).

making a mistake he said, 'Because you have not learned the rules of grammar.' I pressed him, 'Will I be able to read perfectly once I have done so?' When he said yes I asked him to teach me. The next day, when he arrived carrying an Arabic grammar under his arm, Said Agha demanded arrogantly, 'What is that?' to which he responded, 'The book Mistress Nur al-Huda has requested in order to learn grammar.' The eunuch contemptuously ordered, 'Take back your book *Sayyidna Shaikh*. The young lady has no need of grammar as she will not become a judge!' I became depressed and began to neglect my studies, hating being a girl because it kept me from the education I sought. Later, being a female became a barrier between me and the freedom for which I yearned. The memory and anguish of this remain sharp to this day.

When I was nine years old, and had finished memorizing the Koran,[6] my mother celebrated the event with a party, during which I recited verses from the Koran in the presence of my teacher. I was happy on that occasion and later boasted to my friends of my success. It was the first day of joy in our house since the death of my father.

My teacher, Shaikh Ibrahim, had decided to return to Upper Egypt, to his village mosque in Maghagha in the Province of Minya. I mentioned to my mother that he would need a donkey there and that perhaps she might give him one as a reward for his teaching. The day after the party, when he came to say fare-well, she presented him with money to purchase a donkey as well as a letter to Ali Bey Shaarawi, the legal guardian of my brother and me and the trustee of my father's estate, requesting him to assist the *shaikh* in resuming his position as *imam* of the village mosque. I was pleased to see the happiness of my teacher at that moment.

Some people thought I had mastered the Arabic language be-cause I had memorized the Koran but that was not the case. I could read the Koran because the vowels are marked but, unfortunately, I could not read anything else. I went on to study Turkish with eminent teachers like Anwar Afandi, Hasan Afandi Sirri, the famous calligrapher, and Hafiz Afandi, accomplished in elocution and widely celebrated for his recitations of Turkish and Persian poetry. They taught me grammar and calligraphy. I learned to write Ottoman Turkish in two scripts, *riqaa* and *naskh*, which helped me in writing Arabic, as the alphabet was nearly the same. About the same time, an Italian woman began to teach me French and the piano; however, she excelled more in music than language.

I began to buy books from pedlars who came to the door even though I was strictly forbidden to do so. I could not judge the quality of a book. If it was easy to read it was good, otherwise I tossed it in the cupboard. But the books failed to satisfy me and I grew eager to read those of my father who had loved literature and had been surrounded by poets and learned men. At opportune moments I tried various keys to unlock his bookcase which stood in our lesson room, while our two companions kept watch in the corridor. One day when I finally succeeded, I found that some of the books and papers bore the traces of chocolates my father used to keep for us – they had melted over the years. The sight made me sad but curiosity made me reach for the books. I grabbed two at random – the second volume of *Al-Iqd al-Farid (The Unique Necklace)* and the *Diwan* of Abu al-Nasr (collected poems).[7] I still have them to this day.

I had a natural love for poetry and bought every book of poems I came across. My passion increased all the more because of the itinerant poet, Sayyida Khadija al-Maghribiyya,[8] who often visited our house, where she stayed several days at a time in a room set aside especially for her. In the morning I usually found her composing verse while seated on the bed under the mosquito netting. She always obliged my requests for a recitation, but once when I asked her to teach me to compose verse, she answered, 'It is impossible because it requires a knowledge of grammar, morphology, and prosody.' My ignorance pained me and I blamed Said Agha for it.

Sayyida Khadija impressed me because she used to sit with the men and discuss literary and cultural matters. Meanwhile, I observed how women without learning would tremble with embarrassment and fright if called upon to speak a few words to a man from behind a screen. Observing Sayyida Khadija convinced me that, with learning, women could be the equals of men if not surpass them. My admiration for her continued to grow and I yearned to be like her, in spite of her ugly face.

ROUTINES AND EVENTS

Though mornings were devoted to lessons, afternoons were given to play and visits. After lunch, when my brother was taken to his room to rest, I went to the garden and amused myself on the swing, climbing trees and such. If I fell and scratched myself I would apply salves I concocted from the plants in the garden. My brother and I each had a small plot for growing whatever we wanted. In my eagerness to learn about different plants and flowers I was helped by Matta, the gardener, and by Anbar, a mischievous Abyssinian slave whose task in former days had been to make coffee for my father and his guests.

Anbar used to play various tricks on me to get money. One day, he whispered that if piasters were planted they would bear fruit. When I showed interest he took a few of the coins from me and placed them in the ground but warned me to keep quiet so they wouldn't be stolen. After some time had passed, I asked him, 'Why are the piaster trees so long in growing?' and he told me, 'They require more time than other trees.' Finally growing

Huda reclining at home – a playful photograph.

impatient when the soil failed to sprout coins, I asked Matta if people derived much money from what they planted. When he said they did, I asked, 'Then, why haven't my piaster trees borne fruit?' When he inquired, 'What piasters?' I told him my story. He laughed heartily and asked, 'Do gold and silver grow? Anbar has played a trick on you and made off with your money.' It was a lesson to be cautious and not accept everything I was told without question or advice from others.

Another episode made me even more alert. One afternoon, during Ramadan, I was playing in the garden as usual when I noticed a woman, clad in a long black *izar* (cloak) and veil, hastening toward the house. I was surprised to see someone I didn't recognize come during the hours of rest, which was contrary to custom, especially during the month of fasting when calls weren't made before sunset (when the fast was broken). I quickly climbed the stairs to the house after her and asked her to wait in the front hall while I informed my mother of her arrival. Finding my mother asleep, I went to *Umm Kabira*'s room and told her a visitor was waiting downstairs, but she refused to greet her and asked the servant to close the door. I returned rather timidly to the woman who had remained all the while hidden under her heavy veil revealing nothing but her eyes. After sitting politely for some time, I apologized, explaining that my mother and the rest of the household were asleep, and inquired what she wanted.

The woman introduced herself as the widow of a pasha who had been a former neighbour. He had been very wealthy once, she said, but having lost all his money during his last days, he had left her and the children destitute. They often went to bed hungry and so she had come to seek help from my mother. Filled with compassion, I returned to my mother's room to rouse her, but hesitated when I found her fast asleep. Suddenly, I remembered the money I had saved from the allowance my mother and *Umm Kabira* gave me to buy little things for myself. Quietly removing the money from the cupboard next to my mother's bed, I gave it to the woman but was embarrassed by the modest sum of no more than seven pounds. No sooner had I held out my hand than she grabbed the money and fled down the stairs without a word of thanks. I stood still, my heart pounding from amazement, about to regret what I had just done, but I remembered her poor children and decided that in her haste to buy food for them she had forgotten to thank me.

A few days later I heard a neighbour tell my mother about a thief disguised as a woman who called during the hours of rest and claimed to be from a respected old family fallen on hard times, in order to take advantage of the charity of unsuspecting persons. I was upset, not because I had lost the money, but because I had been duped once again.

Usually I played alone in the garden, until late afternoon, when Said Agha came and with a stern look ordered me to change clothes for the daily outing with my brother. Once, my brother appeared and standing hand on hip said peremptorily, 'How shameful that you, a girl, are always outside while I, a boy, pass my time inside.' I responded, 'Tomorrow it will be just the opposite.'

We always began our excursions with Said Agha in fear and trepidation, because if we had done something to upset our nurses they complained to Said Agha, who punished us. He usually took us and our two companions to the Jabalaiyya in Jazira.[9] At the top of the hillock he would command us each to fetch a branch and after listing the complaints that had reached his ears, would strike the palm of our hands until we cried. Afterwards, he took the handkerchiefs from our pockets and wiped our tears saying,

Another view of Qasr al-Nil Bridge with feluccas in the foreground.

'You have received your just reward, but let me warn you not to repeat what you've done or your punishment will be doubled.' Then, suddenly, he would run about playfully like a child while we trailed after him. I tended to forget the unpleasantness because of the fun that followed.

Despite his severity, I liked Said Agha because of his affection and selfless devotion. One afternoon, we were out for a drive in a carriage drawn by a pair of spirited Russian horses that had not been out for days. Just as we were about to cross the Qasr al-Nil Bridge the horses headed straight for the Nile. The terrified Said Agha clutched us in his arms crying, 'Oh, children of my master.' God rewarded his devotion by rescuing us from danger.

When my brother was about seven years old the doctor advised he should be given a pony; apart from being a noble sport, riding made the body strong and stimulated the functioning of the internal organs without being unduly exhausting. I asked for a pony as well, so I could learn to ride like my brother but was told riding was not suitable for girls. The daughter of our neighbour, Lami Bey, an army officer, rode a pony, I quickly answered, and drove a small cart as well. When my mother failed to persuade me girls should not ride she asked me to choose between a pony or a new piano, knowing my passion for music. She won because I chose the piano, but I said to myself, 'I shall get a new piano and ride my brother's pony.'

FEASTS

We used to enjoy the Feasts very much and looked forward to the different ones with great impatience. In the days immediately preceding, we helped the household staff make the ritual foods. We prepared a barley drink called *subiyya* for the *Id al-Saghir* (the Minor Feast) at the end of Ramadan, and on the *Id al-Kabir* (the Major Feast) also called the *Id al-Adha* (the Feast of the Sacrifice of Abraham) slaughtered a sheep and distributed the meat to the poor. For the Tenth of *Muharram, Yaum Ashura* (the anniversary of the slaying of Husain, the grandson of the Prophet Muhammad, at Kerbala) we made *ashura*, a special wheat pudding with nuts and dried fruits. We distributed savoury pastries, *fatta*, and piasters to mark the *Lailat al-Isra wa al-Miraj* (the Night of the Ascension), a solemn and joyous occasion commemorating the night the Prophet Muhammad was lifted through the skies from Arabia to Jerusalem and thence to the heavens.[10]

During feast times we passed the long evenings in large gatherings at home. We would sit on mattresses around a huge lantern – electricity was still rare in Egypt – while our nurses and maids regaled us with stories of their capture and tales of their homelands, till sleep overtook us and we were carried off to bed.

A special holiday treat was the visit of 'The Flower Water Lady', a tall, fat woman with a round face, an awesome spectacle dressed all in white including the *tarha* covering her hair. No sooner had she descended from the phaeton in which she came than she arranged herself on a carpet, spreading out demijohns of flower waters in front of her. Soon the scent of rose, jasmine, lotus, and many other flowers perfumed the air all around. We waited impatiently for the night when we gathered in the main hall, at the head of a crowd stretching up to the front door, while she recounted endless tales in her deep, resonant voice. We huddled closer and closer as she slipped from story to story in answer to our requests. When our eyelids grew heavy and sleep

Huda and friend pose in Egyptian peasant dresses. Dressing up was a favourite pastime in the harem.

forced itself upon us we were carried off to bed swimming in a sea of dreams sparked by this radiant, light-spirited woman who spent her life making the rounds of the great houses of Cairo.

Some feasts were occasions for lively and colourful street celebrations, like the *Mulid-al-Nabi* (the Birthday of the Prophet Muhammad) and the *mulids* of other prophets and saints scattered throughout the year.[11] There was also the festival of the 'cutting of the canal' when the rising Nile waters were ceremonially unleashed each year.[12] We used to go out to the street to watch the merrymaking and buy sweetmeats from the vendors' carts. These were indeed special and happy times.

WOMEN PEDLARS

Numerous women pedlars – not at all like 'The Flower Water Lady' – came periodically to the house. These women, Coptic, Jewish and Armenian, were assisted by young girls carrying wares wrapped in great bundles which they deftly undid in the middle of the hall. Displaying their goods to the members of the household, they urged them to buy various items, claiming that the wife of a certain pasha or bey had purchased a particular article. If anyone inquired about the health of these ladies the pedlars disclosed bits of gossip and were quick to elaborate if their listener appeared eager for more. I didn't like most of these pedlars – although some were quite witty – because they often damaged prominent families through their indiscretions and lies. They also charged exorbitant prices. As a young girl I was cautioned about the pedlars and told of the trouble they could cause. With the unfolding of the years I saw this borne out.

FAMILY FRIENDS

We were always delighted when friends of our father came to call and were touched by their affection and concern for us. I remember, in particular, Thabit Pasha, Uthman Pasha Fauzi, Ahmad Khairi Pasha, Hasan Pasha Abd al-Raziq, Zubair Pasha and Hasan Husni Pasha. Thabit Pasha, a neighbour, had been a long-time friend of our father and his wife was a friend to our mother. My brother and I spent many hours playing with their children in the family garden later occupied by the old Savoy Hotel. From there we could go to the garden of Qattawi Pasha between Sharifain Street and Suliman Pasha Square, where we played with his children.[13]

We used to be intrigued by the house of Uthman Pasha Fauzi, an old fashioned *sarai* with a spacious courtyard full of exotic birds. Pretty white and black slave girls lingered at a *kiosk* in the garden, where we used to play with the Pasha's children. When the Pasha appeared the slaves[14] hurried to greet him with great deference. They prepared coffee and snuff for him while we, along with his children, kissed his hand as he bent towards us in a gentle and dignified manner with his long flowing beard.

I was especially fond of Shaikh Ali al-Laithi who lavished affection on us and often came bringing fruits and sweets. He was poet laureate to Khedive Ismail. He used to hold out his cane for us while we twirled round him reciting verses until we had memorized them. He showed no favouritism between my brother and me, which made me love him all the more. I recall an incident that went straight to my heart. One day when his grandson was with him he asked the young boy whom he would assist when he grew up – the *Hanim* or the *Bey*. The boy replied, 'The *Hanim*,' whereupon the Shaikh said, 'Bravo!'

Zubair Pasha, the infamous old Sudanese slave trader whom I loved as a child, inspired both joy and fear. Whenever I went near him he hugged me so hard I feared my ribs would crack.

Through our father we also came to know a Frenchwoman, Mme Richard, the widow of a hydraulic engineer who had accompanied Ferdinand de Lesseps to work on the Suez Canal.[15] She had arrived in Egypt about the same time with her uncle and only surviving relative, who was also an engineer. There she and Monsieur Richard met, fell in love, and married.

The Continental Savoy Hotel where Huda's husband and other members of the Wafd met the British early in the revolution. Huge throngs greeted the Egyptian nationalists as they descended these stairs.

Monsieur Richard had gone to Upper Egypt to work as an irrigation expert. He had been badly treated and dismissed from his post by my father's predecessor, but was reinstated by my father when he became inspector-general of Upper Egypt. A close bond grew between them until Monsieur Richard died of cholera in the epidemic of 1883, a year before my father died. Afterwards the ties remained alive through Mme Richard. She had eyes as dark as night and coal-black hair. Her charm and refinement, however, surpassed even her beauty. A woman of loyalty and integrity, she showered us with love, giving me the greatest measure which I also returned in abundance. In me she saw a physical resemblance to my father as well as a similarity in character. Mme Richard played an important role in my upbringing, both spiritually and in practical matters.

She stayed with us when my mother travelled to Minya for periodic visits to my father's grave. During her stays she would check the progress of our lessons and encourage us in our studies. Always sad to leave us, she returned often to take us on outings. Her deep affection for me was so apparent that, sometimes, she was asked if I was her daughter, which pleased her immensely. 'So, Huda looks like me,' she would say proudly. As my feelings for her grew, some of the household showed their displeasure. *Umm Kabira* once asked me, 'Why do you love this Christian so much?' to which I replied, that she wasn't a Christian. 'Is she a Muslim then?' 'No,' I responded, 'she's Mme Richard.' Everyone laughed.

VISITING THE PALACE

From my earliest days, I loved and respected Amina Hanim Afandi, the wife of Khedive Taufiq, who was exquisitely gentle and tender.[16] Her majestic air and beauty enthralled me and to this very day she holds a special place in my heart.

My mother took us with her on her occasional visits to the royal palace. She sought assistance from the khedive on certain matters, like the dispute that arose over the custody of my brother and me. My father had designated Ali Shaarawi, the son of his sister, as our legal guardian as well as the trustee of his estate, but this was challenged by a son of my father's brother who felt he should have

Amina Hanim Afandi, 'Mother of Benefactors', Wife of Khedive Taufiq. Huda recalls as a child visiting her in the palace.

custody over us. The princess showed compassion to my worried mother, and helped lighten her cares.

During our visits, the princess would order her slaves to escort my brother and me to the nursery to play with the young princes and princesses. Once, I recall, my brother, who was only four at the time, became intrigued with a particular toy which he refused to part with when the time came to leave. After the attendants made vain efforts to distract his attention, the *kalfa* who supervised the staff asked the princess permission to give him the toy. It was done immediately and my brother departed contented, but I, being older and having a clearer notion of what was proper, was embarrassed.

CHILDHOOD COMPANIONS AND THE FAREWELL

From the time we were very small, my brother and I shared the same friends, nearly all boys, most of whom were the children of our neighbours. The boys remained my companions until I grew up – that is, until I was about eleven – when suddenly I was required to restrict myself to the company of girls and women. I felt a stranger in their world – their habits and notions startled me. Being separated from the companions of my childhood was a painful experience. Their ways left a mark on me.[17]

BETROTHAL TO MY COUSIN

One day when I was dozing while recovering from an illness, I was suddenly roused by excited voices coming from the far end of the room. My mother and 'Aunt' Gazibiyya Hanim, were talking. Gazibiyya Hanim said, 'I have heard that the khedive's family is going to ask for her and if that happens you will have to bow to their will.' She continued, 'However, if necessary, we could arrange a marriage with her cousin (Ali Shaarawi).' My mother said angrily, 'It would be shameful for her to marry a man with children of his own who are older than she is.' Gazibiyya Hanim replied, 'He is the son of her father's sister and "lord and master" of all.' My mother answered, 'We shall see what happens.'

The room began to spin and the remarks of the nurses and slaves made whenever my cousin called came echoing back. After announcing his arrival in the routine manner, they would add, 'Go and greet your husband.' It angered me but I dismissed it as a mischievous taunt. When the truth behind it became apparent, I wept long and hard, and the shock caused my illness to worsen and persist for a long time afterwards.

My cousin began to come to Cairo with greater frequency and passed many hours in the company of my mother. At times, I feared they were about to reach an agreement over my future but my forebodings vanished when I detected anger in my mother's speech. Gradually I paid less attention to the matter and it eventually slipped from my mind altogether.

One day, when my mother summoned me, I found a casket of jewels lying open in front of her; she asked me to select some pieces in fulfilment of a vow she had made for the recovery of my illness. I chose a splendid diamond necklace and bracelet and rushed to show them to *Umm Kabira* so she could share my joy.[18]

Not long after that, *Umm Kabira* died. Profoundly saddened by her death, I put on the ring she had given me for memorizing the Koran and have never removed it since. If she had not passed away, I might have discovered certain truths but, as it was, there was no one to explain things I could not understand on my own.

After the forty days of mourning passed, I noticed that when friends came to call on my mother, Fatanat would fetch the jewels to show the guests. When this was repeated a number of times, I became dismayed and remarked people would begin to think we were *nouveau riche* and had never before seen such things. The maid scowled but said nothing. I later observed Fatanat and the slaves embroidering squares of silk with silver and gold thread, and learned that *shurs*, as they were called, were customarily presented to friends and relations at the signing of a marriage contract. When I inquired who was getting married, I was told it was the daughter of a pasha in whose household my mother's maid had once been employed.

Not long after that, repairs began on our house. During that time my mother decided to pass the winter months in Helwan and so she took a small villa east of the *jabal*, where the sanitorium is now, but which at that time was still a barren stretch leading to the rocky escarpment. When we left for Helwan, I was still ignorant of what was happening.

I marvelled at Helwan, which owed its splendour to Khedive Taufiq, who had adopted it as his winter retreat. Immediately afterwards, other royalty and the aristocratic families began to flock there during the winter season or for short outings. It became a pleasant haven from the capital. People frequented the theatre and casino and the garden pavilions where Shaikh Salama Hijazi performed theatricals. Music played and swaying lanterns illuminated the night. The theatre and concerts gave me great pleasure. In the days when women were still veiled, Helwan offered a more relaxed atmosphere in place of their routine seclusion in Cairo.[19]

After we were there for some time one of my friends came to spend a few days with us. One afternoon as I was taking her on a promenade to show her the delightful sights, we were startled by the appearance of Said Agha, who was accompanying some gentlemen. 'Where are you going?' he scowled. 'Return to the house at once!' We submitted to his command and retraced our steps. Upon entering the house I was surprised to find that the woman who had instructed me in Turkish had arrived in our absence. She was standing in the hall, still wearing her *tarha* and carrying another one in her hand. When she handed me a Koran I grew perplexed. Said Agha entered escorting Ali Pasha Fahmi, the husband of a second cousin, and Saad al-Din Bey, an officer in the Palace Guard, who later married Gazibiyya Hanim. When they came towards me, I hastened to my room thoroughly bewildered, but they followed and I retreated to the window, where I stood with my back to them. To my utter astonishment, Ali Pasha Fahmi announced. 'The son of your father's sister wants your hand in marriage and we are here on his behalf.'

Only then did I understand the reason for the various preparations underway in the house, as well as a number of other mysteries. With my back to the men, I cried without speaking or moving. I stood sobbing by the window for nearly three hours. Occasionally passers-by glanced up sympathetically. Eventually Ali Pasha Fahmi and Saad al-Din Bey asked, 'Whom do you wish to designate as your *wakil* to sign the marriage contract?'[20] I said nothing, and after a long silence, Said Agha whispered in my ear, 'Do you wish to disgrace the name of your father and destroy your poor mother who is weeping in her sickbed and might not survive the shock of your refusal?' Upon hearing these words, which pierced my heart, I replied, 'Do whatever you want,' and rushed immediately to my mother's room scraping my head on a nail on the side of the door in my haste. Bleeding and about to faint, I must have been a pitiful sight. My friend and others around me wept.

My spirit was broken and I spent the rest of my stay in Helwan with my eyes full of tears. I began to stroll on the lonely escarpment instead of the gardens with their concert pavilions and theatres. My two young companions used to accompany me, but I often left them to wander off in the distance alone, while I pondered how I could avoid the marriage. When I shared my thoughts with my companions, the elder, who believed in sorcery, said a magic spell would be cast upon me so that I would accept tomorrow what I rejected today. I tried in vain to disabuse her of this.

When we returned to Cairo, I discovered great changes. The house had been repainted and the furniture redone. The dressmaker had begun work on my wedding gown but I did not let her try it on me. I ignored the other endless preparations right up to the time the wedding day approached and strings of lights were hung in the garden. My mother, I noticed, was given to frequent outbursts of anger, the way she had been about the time of my betrothal, but I did not know the reason for her ill-temper and did not inquire.

I was deeply troubled by the idea of marrying my cousin whom I had always regarded as a father or older brother deserving my fear and respect (as I had been previously made to understand). I grew more upset when I thought of his wife and three daughters who were all older than me, who used to tease me saying, 'Goodday, stepmother!' When my brother and I were small and our guardian–cousin called on us, I did not find him gentle. He was especially abrupt and curt with me, but treated my brother better. All of this alienated me from him.

My mother surprised me one day when she came to my room with a document which she asked me to read aloud to her, adding that my future husband had refused to sign it. It stipulated that my cousin, upon his marriage with me, would have no further relations with the mother of his children, nor would he ever take another wife. Until then, always mindful of his wife and children, I was certain that the marriage would not take place, but after reading the document reality struck home and I wept. My mother, thinking I was upset at my cousin's refusal to sign said, 'Everything has been done to secure his written consent but all efforts have failed. The preparations for the wedding have been completed and the invitations issued. It would be a disgrace to stop the wedding now. Accept things as they are for the moment, my daughter, and, God willing, in the future he will agree to these conditions. This is your destiny and God is your guide.' I didn't utter a word; when my mother pressed me to speak, I said only, 'Do as you please,' and left in tears.

I had known nothing of the rooms in the house prepared for me following my marriage until the day my mother herself took me to see them. I must confess, I had never before seen such sumptuous furnishings. I grew excited and I inquired if they were to be my very own.[21] When my companion witnessed this she said triumphantly, 'Didn't I predict that you would be won over by magic?' Her remark plunged me into gloom not so much because I took it seriously, but because the beauty of the rooms had elevated my spirits for a fleeting moment.

THE WEDDING

The three nights of wedding festivities with their music and gaiety expelled my melancholy and kept me from thinking of what was to come. I laughed and was merry along with my friends, so much so that the household interpreted my earlier behaviour as nothing more than the ordinary display of fears common to prospective brides.[22]

On the night of the wedding ceremony, the rapt attention focused upon me, especially by my friends, increased my joy so that I almost leaped with delight while I donned my wedding dress embroidered in thread of silver and gold. I was spellbound by the diamonds and other brilliant jewels that crowned my head and sparkled on my bodice and arms. All of this dazzled me and kept me from thinking of anything else. I was certain I would remain forever in this raiment, the centre of attention and admiration.

Presently, the singing girls appeared to escort me. My attendants supported me while the heavy jewels pressed down on my head and the wedding dress hung heavy on my small frame. I walked between rows of bright candles with rich scents wafting in the air, to the grand salon where I found a throng of women – Egyptians and Europeans – in elegant gowns with jewels glittering on their heads, bosoms and arms. They all turned and looked at me with affection. When I raised my head to ease the heavy tiara back a little I heard a woman's voice whispering, 'My daughter, lower your head and eyes.' I then sat down on the bridal throne surrounded by flickering candles and decorated with flowers, fancying I was in another world.

Some of the European guests placed bouquets of roses and other blossoms in my hands or at my feet. I failed to understand the feelings of sympathy these women had for my marrying at such a tender age. A pair of maids brought the shawls presented to me by my mother's friends. Removing them from their velvet packets one by one, they unfolded the shawls and spread them out one after the other announcing the name of the donor, repeating in succession, 'May bounty be granted also to her.' After all had been laid in a great pile they were bundled and carried away.

Next a dancer appeared and started to perform in front of me. She then made the rounds of the guests dancing in front of the women one at a time. They would take out coins, moisten them with their tongues and paste them on the dancer's forehead and cheeks.

Suddenly, a commotion erupted outside the great hall. The dancer rushed out emitting a string of *zaghrudas*, the tremulous trills hanging in the air after her. To the roll of drums the women hastened out of the room or slipped behind curtains while the eunuch announced the approach of the bridegroom.

In an instant, the delicious dream vanished and stark reality appeared. Faint and crying, I clung to the gown of a relation – the wife of Ahmad Bey Hijazi – who was trying to flee like the others and I pleaded, 'Don't abandon me here! Take me with you.' My French tutor who was at my side embraced me and cried along with me murmuring, 'Have courage, my daughter, have courage.' Mme Richard, supporting me on the other side, wept as she tried to console me with tender words. Then a woman came and lowered a veil of silver thread over my head like a mask concealing the face of a condemned person approaching execution. At that moment, the bridegroom entered the room. After praying two *rakaas* on a mat of red velvet embossed with silver he came to me and, lifting the veil from my face, kissed me on the forehead. He led me by the hand to the bridal throne and took his place beside me. All the while, I was trembling like a branch in a storm. The groom addressed a few words to me but I understood nothing. When the customary goblets of red sorbet were offered, I was unable to taste the ritual drink. Finally, my new husband took me by the hand. In my daze I knew not where I was being led.

The next morning when I looked out of my window, the big tent adorned with fine carpets and embroidered hangings was gone. Gone also were the bright lights that had enchanted me the night before. I had been certain they would all remain a long time. How desolate I was when I saw the work of the hand of destruction! Nothing remained on the grounds where the tent had been raised – not a single tree of the many trees I loved, all of which held special memories for me. Gone was the apricot tree that shaded me and bent low offering me its fruits. Its purple flowers gave the garden a special beauty perfuming the air all round, even in the house. Nothing remained of the orange trees whose blossoms wrapped the ground in a fleece of white flowers which we used for making perfumed garlands. Uprooted were the prune trees and the magnolia tree whose large white blooms I plucked for my mother the moment their petals unfolded. Nothing remained of the *daqn al-basha*, 'the pasha's beard', with its delicate tiny fruit we called *tuffah al-walida*, 'mother's apples'. Gone were the Indian jasmine, the Arabian jasmine, the basil, and the pear trees, and the *luisa* trees whose leaves we crushed in our fingers to extract the lemony scent. Not even a *sitt al-mistihiyya*, 'the shy lady', was spared. Its leaves, curled up and closed whenever we touched them, shrinking from us with shyness, we thought.

I loved all those trees – the big and the small – and swung from their branches in my girlhood. They had been planted by my father who had loved them as I had, and who had cared for them and enjoyed eating their fruit. All had become lost remnants of grandeur. All were sacrificed at the call of a single night, a night I had fancied would last in all its beauty and majesty forever, a night when my sorrows and agonies had vanished. But it faded like an enchanting dream. Bitter reality followed. I wept for my trees. I wept for my childhood and for my freedom. I saw in this barren garden a picture of life – the life I would live cut off from everything that had delighted me and consoled me in my melancholy childhood. I turned from the window with a heavy heart and avoided the garden for a long, long time, unable to bear these aching reveries.

A NEW BRIDE

For a long time I did not fully appreciate that my new status as a married woman required a solemn demeanour and obliged me to appear with the poise of a perfect lady, for owing to my youth I was still under the influence of a child's life and subject to its rulings. I would play whenever I had the chance. In the afternoon or evening, when I heard my husband's footsteps on the stairs, I was the first among the women to escape behind a curtain (custom

Ali Pasha Shaarawi, husband of Huda.

ordained that a woman hide at the approach of a man other than her husband). Those who witnessed the scene would laugh and force me to greet my husband, which I did only with trepidation.

My hesitations and fears began to disappear as I grew closer to my husband. We possessed ties of kinship and after our marriage he showed me kindness. For my part, I was able to offer him companionship. However, that state did not last long. Only a few months had passed when I noticed a certain strangeness come over him. His treatment of me changed but I had no idea why. If I wanted to visit a relative or friend he would forbid me to go. If someone called on me he would interrogate me about our conversation. If I amused myself at the piano while he had visitors he would send an order to stop. I felt he was limiting me unjustly and grew depressed and restless. As boredom overtook me I wept profusely, with and without reason. I began to carry a book around with me to camouflage the source of my unhappiness, so if I was caught crying I could say I was reading a sad story. My husband, among others, observed my melancholy. He did not understand it and asked me the cause.

Meanwhile, I began to notice unusual behaviour on his part. When I saw him pray with greater frequency I would say, 'You must have done something that calls for repentance, but God will not heed your supplications.' He had a troubled look but I did not know why.

One day I heard my mother speak to my husband in a loud, angry voice. Then she summoned me inquiring about a document my husband had given me, but I had no recollection of it. My husband turned and said, 'It is in the envelope I handed you the morning after our wedding.' Then I recalled he had given me a sealed envelope on which was written, 'To be kept with the Lady'. I had merely placed it in the wardrobe, not knowing what it contained. When I retrieved the envelope, my mother asked me to open it, and read the document aloud to her. It was a declaration by Ali Shaarawi freeing his slave–concubine upon his marriage to me and committing himself thereafter to a monogamous union. It was a legal document, duly signed by two witnesses. My mother, saying nothing, took the document for safekeeping.[23]

From time to time, when my mother journeyed to Upper Egypt to visit my father's grave, she stayed with my mother-in-law. It was there that my husband's former slave–concubine and daughters lived. Not long after the above incident, my mother and I went to stay with my husband's mother. When we arrived, she appeared on the veranda to welcome us, as was her custom, but she was in a peculiar mood. Fatanat, who was in the service of my mother-in-law at the time, greeted me obsequiously even bending down to kiss my hand. I was taken aback by this unusual behaviour.

I followed my mother into the sitting room, where we removed our *izars*, and sat down. Suddenly, she asked me why I had hidden the real cause of my unhappiness, whereupon I asked her what she meant. 'Are you still trying to keep the truth from me?' she asked. 'I know all about your husband's return to his former slave who is about to have a child.' When I heard that I clapped my hands with joy. I rushed to my companion and confidante and told her the news that would bring the end to my misery. Amazed by my reaction, my mother demanded to know if I was feinting joy to conceal my real feelings and hide the fact that I had known about matters all along. I swore that it was the first I had heard of it and assured her that my happiness was genuine. I confessed that I had been in misery and that my constant tears were proof of it.

A few minutes later, I heard my husband clap to signal his presence, as was his custom, when he approached the hall. I rushed to congratulate him on the imminent birth and wished him a boy. I knew he wanted a son to name him Hasan, after his father. He showed discomfort when I went on to say, 'Do you remember I used to say you must have done something wrong to be evoking God's mercy so often? I was right. It is now clear. Adieu!' Fifteen months had not yet elapsed since the wedding.

Afterward, he tried to effect a reconciliation, promising to fulfil his obligations and whatever else might be requested of him. My mother was highly agitated. For some time we believed, according to the document I have mentioned, that I was divorced. However, we later discovered we had not properly understood it. The document stipulated that my husband relinquished the right to take any wife other than me. During those days of misunderstanding and controversy, I spent my time in play, taking little notice of the discussions between my mother and my husband. I was determined not to return to him whatever happened.

◀PART THREE▶

A SEPARATE LIFE

1892–1900

LESSONS AGAIN

The seven years I remained apart from my husband was a time for new experiences and for growing into adulthood. I requested my former teacher of French and piano to resume our lessons, and another tutor was appointed for drawing and painting. Still eager to perfect my Arabic grammar, I asked the husband of a relation to arrange for an Azhar *shaikh* to instruct me. As our household was conservative I took care to request an elderly teacher who would be permitted entry into the harem. Sometime later, Shaikh Musa from the Qasr al-Ali mosque was presented to me. From the beginning, however, he encountered difficulties when he came for lessons. The eunuchs, for example, would fail to have him properly conducted to the lesson room. Increasingly frustrated by the treatment he received, the *shaikh* departed one day, never to return, leaving me with the impossible task of teaching myself Arabic grammar. The French lessons proceeded without interruption, however, and so I am far better at French than Arabic.

I loved music very much, especially European music, and my appreciation deepened when I began to attend concerts at the Khedival Opera House where I shared a private box with my friend, Adila Hanim Nabarawi.[1] Meanwhile, I spent nearly every evening at home playing piano pieces from memory. As soon as dinner was over I would go to the piano and play long into the night, losing myself in the music. I would leave the salon, my eyes wet with tears of rapture and the music resounding in my ears till sleep came.

COMPANIONSHIP

Good fortune came my way when a girl my age, the daughter of a neighbour who was an official in the Egyptian Ministry of Defence, came from France to stay with her family in Cairo. My new – and strong-willed – friend was well educated and shared many of my interests, including the piano and French literature. The hours slipped away while we read novels and poetry in French together, and if there were words we didn't understand we would search the *Larousse Dictionary*. In that way I perfected my French.

My affection grew when I learned about my friend's unhappy home life. Her mother had died quite a while ago and her father, after remarrying, had had more children. My friend's aunts lived in the house with her father and stepmother but the women did not get along. My friend caused resentment if she showed too much attention either to her aunts or her stepmother. Her father was a man who did not wish to hear any complaints, and so she found no one but me to listen to her troubles and offer sympathy. She often came to me for support to help her endure her life at home. Except for Fatanat who found ways to offend my friend, no one bothered us. We took special pleasure in the company of Mme Richard who often joined us while we read, played the piano, or embroidered. When we were blue, her blithe spirit and soothing words revived us as the morning dew revives wilting blossoms.

Mme Richard possessed many fine qualities, including generosity to the point of self-sacrifice. She loved those who loved me and disliked those who did not like me or hurt me. Unfortunately, she was also an obsessive person with strong likes and dislikes and could be roused to jealousy over the love I showed others. Her friends liked her very much but her marked candour prevented many from appreciating her true worth. Fatanat disliked Mme Richard on account of the affection she showered upon me and her

Huda with Adila Nabarawi and her young daughter, Saiza.

protectiveness toward me. Whenever the maid scolded me Mme Richard was quick to come to my defence, and often I feared she would actually strike Fatanat, which would have led to disastrous consequences. Eventually, Fatanat undermined Mme Richard's position in the eyes of my mother, who began complaining that I clung excessively to her. During those times, when various persons caused me anguish by trying to pressure me into reconciling with my husband, Mme Richard stood loyally at my side.

ATTEMPTS AT RECONCILIATION

I recall the day Zubair Pasha came to see me inquiring why I did not return to my husband and tend to his needs. He remarked that my behaviour was not fitting for a daughter of Sultan Pasha and added, 'Do you know that your husband has the right to force you to return to him?[2] Do you understand that your refusal is a disgrace, all the more so because he is your cousin?' He went on in this brusque and insensitive manner while I listened silently to words I did not deserve. When he noticed the tears falling from my eyes he said, 'I am talking to you in this way because your father was like a brother and I consider myself to be speaking with his tongue.' That forced me to reply. 'My father would not have permitted me to listen to such words! I have done no wrong. My husband is the guilty one. Yet, in spite of that, if I knew he needed me I would not hesitate for a moment to sacrifice myself to him but, in fact, he does not need me. He lives with his former slave who bears him a child every year. It is enough that I don't question him about the matter and am able to bear all of this. I am sure my father would not condone his daughter's suffering over this, for he was just and compassionate.' With that I left him. The following day, he sent his wife to apologize for his severity.

Some days later, I heard that Shaikh Ali al-Laithi also wished to serve as mediator between my husband and me. I knew the matter troubled him deeply and that he did not hold me accountable. Despite his poor health and advanced age, he bore the hardship of

The Cairo Opera House built by Khedive Ismail in 1869, called the Khedivial Opera House in Huda's day where she and her friend Adila Hanim Nabarawi, had a screened box. Women in those days entered by a separate staircase.

travel to Upper Egypt every year to visit my father's grave, until finally he was no longer strong enough to perform his duty to a friend. I was upset because I loved him very much and feared if he treated me as Zubair Pasha had, my love and respect for him would diminish. Fortunately, he never appeared.

There were many other attempts at mediation by relatives and friends, who used various tactics. My husband himself frequently came to make entreaties, sometimes gently, sometimes sternly. I always spoke to him in a calm and reasoned way, reminding him of his obligations to his children and their mother. I told him, 'There is nothing that ties me to you but the bond of kinship and gratitude for your services toward the family,' adding, 'I am certain you want me back to ease your conscience. You may think you have hurt me but you have a duty toward your children that requires you to live with them. I can assure you that you contribute toward my happiness by remaining with them and their mother.' He protested that only love caused him to insist upon my return and, at times, I detected signs of true sadness on his face.

SOJOURNS IN ALEXANDRIA

The repeated entreaties for a reconciliation and my own efforts at self-restraint wore down my health and sent me to bed for a few months. Our friend and family doctor, Alwi Bey, advised me at the approach of summer to leave for Alexandria to take advantage of the fresh air and sea bathing. The prospect pleased me – I had an instinctive longing for the sea – and I spent that summer at Ramleh on the Mediterranean near Alexandria with my mother, brother, and other members of the household.[3] It was the first time I had ventured outside Cairo since our stay in Helwan. Three months after this visit ended we returned again for a short holiday. My love for the sea increased and my health improved.

The next year as soon as summer drew near I was eager to return to our seaside retreat, but my husband, when he learned of this, tried to prevent my departure unless I accepted a reconciliation. When no signs of that were forthcoming he withheld payment of the money for my expenses in Alexandria and thus put an end to my plans. I feigned indifference but, in fact, craved the sea air and pleasant isolation and went so far as to buy a sponge which

I sniffed from time to time to remind me of the sea. Once as I held the sponge to my nose, inhaling the briny scent, my 'Aunt' saw me and immediately understood my feelings. She told my mother who, on the next day, went to Alexandria and rented a house with her own funds. I was then allowed to depart accompanied by my 'Aunt'.

It was arranged that I would receive a monthly stipend of fifty pounds, to be taken from my own income, to pay the salaries for my tutors and servants, the expenses for food, clothing, the horse and carriage, and entertaining.[4] It was adequate for me in Cairo where I carefully tended to matters myself but in Alexandria, where Said Agha took charge of purchases and expenditures, it never lasted the month owing to his carelessness and extravagance. I was therefore hard-pressed to make ends meet and faced endless inconveniences. Once when I was invited to attend a birthday party for the son of one of my friends, the end of the month was near and I had no more than three pounds left. With this I had to buy a gift for the child and also a new cloak for myself because my *izar* was frayed at the hem where it brushed against the sand. In those days, women wore *izars* over their dresses when they went out, and at their destination would leave them in a special room set aside for the purpose. It would have been an insult to my hostess if I, coming from a wealthy family, appeared in a worn-out cloak. As I pondered my dilemma, the maid announced the arrival of a pedlar of fine stuffs at the door and inquired if I would like to view her wares in the garden. A swathe of black woollen cloth caught my eye and I asked the price. Only twenty-five piasters a yard, I was delighted to hear, and it solved my problem. After buying the cloth I gave it to my 'Aunt', asking her to call for the seamstress who took twenty piasters for a day's work. The seamstress suggested a pattern, and with further instructions from my 'Aunt' and myself she set to work. With the rest of the money I went to Alexandria and bought a gift for the boy. At the party the other women praised my *izar*, the only one of its kind, inquiring about the fabric and who had made it. I told them it was a new material that withstood wear from sand and moisture. My friends copied my *izar* and soon there were many like it. No one knew the story behind the cloak. They thought it was the latest style and it continued to be fashionable for some time.

I liked Ramleh because its long stretch of beach gave me a place to exercise and relax. I also enjoyed going into Alexandria to call on friends or make excursions to the new modern department stores, despite the continual grumbling and fussing I had to endure from Said Agha. I remember the first shopping trip to Chalon. The mere prospect of it threw the entire household into an uproar and provided the main topic of discussion and heated debate for days. They looked upon me as if I were about to violate the religious law or commit some other crime. After considerable persuasion on my part, however, my mother gave in to my wishes and, along with everyone else around me, issued endless orders and instructions for my correct behaviour. They insisted it was not proper for me to go alone, but I must be accompanied by Said Agha and my maids. The day of the outing, Said Agha made doubly sure I was completely hidden with wraps and veil.

When I entered Chalon, the staff and clientele were visibly taken aback by this veiled apparition and her retinue. In the lead Said Agha stared into the surrounding faces, silently warning them to

Qasr al-Nil, a fashionable modern shopping street in Cairo, site of early department stores like the one Huda first visited in Alexandria.

Carriage conveying a lady with yashmak (Turkish style veil) at Ramleh near Alexandria, where Huda summered.

look the other way, while the maids followed in the rear. The eunuch proceeded straight to the store manager and brusquely demanded the place for the harem. We were led to the department for women's apparel, behind a pair of screens hastily erected to obscure me from view. A saleswoman was assigned to wait on me and to bring whatever I wished. One of her young assistants – amazed by the proceedings – asked about me and my family. Said Agha attacked her with ferocious looks and immediately complained about her impertinence to the manager. She trembled in fear while the other assistants covered their smiles with their hands. The manager was about to dismiss the young assistant then and there. I intervened, however, and asked him not to. I was thoroughly ashamed of the whole scene. Whenever I went shopping the procedure would be repeated all over again until one day I finally persuaded my mother to accompany me. She was then quick to see the advantages of shopping in person. Not only was there a wide range of goods to choose from but there was money to be saved through wise spending. From then on she resolved to do her own shopping and permitted me to do my own as well.

PORTRAIT OF THE HARD LIFE OF A WOMAN

One day at the end of summer, after returning from Alexandria, my mother summoned me to read aloud a card the servant had just delivered to her – a message from a foreign woman who was waiting at the door. When I read out the name, Atiyya Saqqaf, my mother was elated and immediately ordered her servant to bid the woman enter. She was a relative from Stamboul, about whom I knew nothing. After fervent embraces, my mother introduced me to a woman of striking beauty, about thirty years old. We sat for a while, until I went to my own quarters and left them alone. Later, the woman came to my room and began talking with me as if we were old friends. I, being naturally reserved, was put off by her informality and intimate questions. She stayed with us for a week, continuing to press me about personal matters and give her own opinions. I began avoiding her whenever I could. However, I concealed my displeasure and when she departed I gave her some roses from our garden as a token of farewell.

Some months later a letter arrived from Madina thanking us for our hospitality. Atiyya Hanim Saqqaf wrote that the time at our house had passed like a dream and as a memento she had kept the roses I had given her. She told us about her visit to the tomb of the Prophet Muhammad, God bless him and upon him be salvation. She had separated from her husband, for reasons she was unable to explain, but would remain in Madina for a year until her youngest son was weaned. Then she would give him and her other children over to the custody of their father and return to Stamboul where her brother lived.

Saddened by this news, my mother asked me to write a letter on her behalf inviting her to come to our house, where she would find a sympathetic 'mother' and 'sister'. She arrived about a year later. Her face was a mirror of grief and desperation that had undermined her health. Her suffering caused me to draw close to her. When I asked why she had faded after having been so radiant she started to speak of her life.

> I was born of a Circassian mother and a Turkish father. My father, who was wealthy, married my mother after his first wife had failed to bear him children. My mother gave him a boy and a girl. Later, he died after losing his fortune, leaving only the large house where we lived and the garden. My mother was a young woman at her

wits' end. After some time she was introduced to a suitable man whom she soon married. He treated her well and cared for us like a father.

There was a neighbouring family of ordinary means who had a bright young son, a little older than I. He began to grow fond of me. My mother used to say, 'I shall arrange a marriage between Atiyya and him.' We grew up expecting this. When he finished school, he began to work for the government and was posted outside Stamboul. Afterwards, I no longer saw him. Some time later my mother heard he was going to marry a girl in the town where he worked. She became angry.

Then one day my step-father arrived with a dark-skinned stranger who asked for my hand in marriage. After ascertaining that he was not already married and would not oblige me to leave her side and live abroad, my mother consented.

When news of the impending marriage reached our neighbour's son, he hastened to Stamboul. He tried to dissuade her from going through with the plans for my marriage. He confessed that he had been married only briefly. He said he had never stopped loving me. His love was so strong that if my mother deprived him of me he

Drawing of Huda in her teens done in the Harem by her friend, Atiyya Saqqaf, clearly an accomplished artist.

Atiyya Saqqaf with the son from whom she was separated.

would take his life. I, for my part, still loved the man and wished to marry him. The two of us concocted a plan. At nightfall on the eve of my wedding, I was to jump out of the bathroom window which was close to the ground. Unfortunately, my attempted escape was discovered and I was brought back to the house again.

I cannot describe my anxieties and how much I feared my husband the night of our wedding. I believed dark men ate white people. Nevertheless, he gained my affection and later when he decided to return home to Arabia, I insisted upon going with him. My mother accompanied us as well. Once in the Hidjaz, it was indeed confirmed that my husband did not have another wife. My mother, forebodings eased, returned after some time home to Stamboul. My husband and I lived in harmony for three years. I gave birth to a girl, although he preferred a son.

My husband went to Mecca every year for the *haj* (pilgrimage). One year when he lingered I became suspicious. I began to open his letters, struggling to read them despite my poor Arabic. I learned that he had taken another wife. When he returned, I confronted him. In anger, I returned to my mother in Stamboul. I discovered after my marriage that our neighbour's son had fallen ill and eventually died. I was told he had never ceased to think of me, saying 'Tell her I shall never forget her.' I was deeply saddened.

My anger against my husband who had been unfaithful and not cared that I had pledged my life to him continued to rage. He had disregarded that I was young and a stranger to his country. The following summer, my husband arrived in Turkey. He made great efforts to achieve a reconciliation. He explained that he had married the daughter of a wealthy uncle to save the family patrimony from being broken up. Eventually, I consented to return with him to Madina and later gave birth to a boy.

However, it became clear before long that he would not be satisfied with one wife, or even two. I was told he had worked as a young man on ships owned by an uncle, a prosperous merchant in Indonesia. During the annual *haj* season he worked on the pilgrim ships bound for Arabia. He would marry a woman aboard ship and divorce her upon arrival. His marriages were so numerous he couldn't count them nor did he know the number of children he had. Meanwhile, I found him going after servant girls, in the house. Once when I caught him outright he began to beat the girl, pretending she had assaulted him.

Life continued like that for some time when he became gravely ill and everyone – even the doctors – eventually withdrew from him. I spent months at his side, nursing him day and night. He once asked how he could reward me for all I was doing whereupon I asked him to take me to visit the tomb of the Prophet, God bless him and upon him be salvation, when he recovered and he gave me his word.

No sooner was my husband able to stand on his feet again, not without the support of a cane, however, than he journeyed alone to Mecca to remain there with his second wife. I was badly shaken. After some time, he summoned me to make the journey to the holy shrine at Madina. Yet when I arrived in Mecca, my husband ignored me and the children. We made the journey to Madina as planned but when we reached our destination I did not dismount the camel with my husband but proceeded with the children to the house of an aunt. I sent him a letter requesting a divorce and insisted that our infant son stay with me until he was weaned. My husband concurred. The children remained with me for the stipulated period. I then delivered them to my husband's *wakil* and the agent gave them to their father.[5]

Next I made preparations for my departure and hired two camels for myself and my maid. A caravan of Turkish soldiers taking the mail agreed to let us travel with them to Mecca on condition we dress like men. My aunt urged me to stay in Madina, warning of bedouin attacks on the caravans. In my despair and suffering, I was determined to leave at all costs. We set out from Madina and after covering several leagues by nightfall pitched camp outside the walls of a large dwelling. The master informed us the bedouin had closed off the mountain pass because the Turkish government had failed to pay them their customary tribute. The soldiers turned to me and said, 'We shall take you back to Madina before continuing as we cannot guarantee your safety.' I replied, 'Let us go forward. Whatever befalls you, befalls me.' That night as dinner was being prepared, a group of veiled bedouin passed by our encampment. We invited them to partake of our meal but they rode on without answering. This was an unfriendly gesture that confirmed what we had heard about their hostility.

The following morning we arose before dawn and set out. We had been crossing the desert for some time when we met a party of bedouin who shouted orders to stop. The Turkish soldiers asked if I could gallop. I gave free rein to my camel as gun shots signalled the battle was on. In an instant, what seemed like thousands of bedouin appeared on the high plateau and descended upon us like lightning. They had forced us to a standstill and had begun to direct their fire at us when I shouted out to the Turkish soldiers, 'Stop! There are two women with you! Do not sacrifice them!' A soldier shouted back, 'How can we sacrifice our honour and the purse and weapons of the Ottoman government?' By imploring them to stop I revealed my fear of death. The soldiers painfully surrendered and were divested of their weapons and money.

When the bedouin recognized two women, they made us dismount. They opened my saddle bag and removed the silver coins I had brought for expenses, as well as a string of fake pearls which appeared valuable in the glistening sun. They ordered us to follow them. When I asked where they were taking us they said, 'To our tents to pay you honour and that you may partake of our repast.' One of them added, 'We are going to devour you!'

When I feigned fright, the chief said, 'Do not fear, oh *Sharifa*, we wish to honour you and receive your *baraka*.' When examining my possessions they had discovered my seal and my children's seals carrying the name of my former husband, a descendant of the Prophet, may God bless him and upon him be salvation. The bedouin revere the descendants of the Prophet. My former husband had also always been generous with them.[6]

Unable to tread the stones and thorns, I was carried to the encampment on the back of my servant. The chief led us to his tent where his women welcomed me. They gathered round me and touched me all over exclaiming, 'How beautiful you are!' I understood they wanted to know if anything was concealed under my garments. When they came upon a solid object I told them it was the Holy Koran which was always with me. To prove I was speaking the truth, they asked me to remove it and read some *ayas* to them, which I did. The bedouin slaughtered animals for us and fêted us lavishly.

Early the next morning, the chief appeared to wish me good day and said, 'Oh, *Sharifa*, you have honoured us. You and your companions may now go in peace.' I replied, 'How can we proceed when you have taken all we possess? I fear we shall be halted along the way by bedouin not as noble and kind as you and your people.'

He answered, 'Our home is your home. You may remain with us as long as you wish.' I said, 'I am awaited in Mecca and my relations will grow anxious if I do not appear.' He asked, 'What then can I do for you?' and I answered, 'Ride with us and protect us.' He laughed and asked, 'Do you wish to deliver me over to the Turkish authorities who have put a price on my head?' I told him, 'I shall be responsible for your safety. I give my promise that no harm shall befall you.' He replied, 'I pledge to protect you, I am at your service.' I asked him to bring enough money for the journey, which I would repay upon arrival in Mecca. I also requested the return of the mail pouches and unloaded rifles to the soldiers so the Ottoman authorities would not discipline them.

With the bedouin chief as our guide, the caravan set out once more. Whenever we approached an encampment he would hasten forward in greeting and in an instant we would be welcomed with drums and flutes. The nomads would seek my blessing, holding out their ailing children for me to touch, as they had great faith in the miraculous powers of the descendants of the Prophet. Near Mecca, the chief dismounted and dug a hole in a small hillock. A Turkish soldier told me he had buried a rifle – undoubtedly one of the recently pilfered ones – and he intended to report it immediately upon arrival in Mecca. 'Do not,' I said, 'I have promised him protection. If it were not for his trust in me, you and your companions would not be alive now.' I made him swear he would not reveal what he had seen. As we made our entry into Mecca, the chief disappeared from sight.

After returning to my house, I collected a bundle of clothing and other items, including the garlic I had promised the bedouin women. At nightfall there came a knock on the door. The bedouin chief had come to settle accounts for the journey and to collect the promised gifts. When I paid him his due, he thanked me, wished me well, and pledged to remain forever in my service. He excused the deeds of his tribesmen by explaining they were poor. When the Turkish government cut off payments of money and grain, they were forced to block the caravan routes to put pressure on the authorities. Otherwise, they would die of starvation. The chief took his leave. On the following day I left for Jeddah and thence to Egypt.

After hearing this sad tale I was moved to treat Atiyya Hanim like a sister, to gain her love and confidence. She was correct, sincere and loyal, and lavish in her love for me. Yet, she was also demanding in her love and wished to monopolize me. She could not bear it if I gave my attention to anyone else, if I left her sight for long or failed to seek her advice. I began to rebel against her attempts to control me. Often we quarrelled and she would threaten to leave, but these outbursts always ended in reconciliation because I would give in to her. I so wanted her to be happy.

My friend became a recluse. She spent day and night in her room passing her time in needlework. If she was present when frequent women callers visited the house, she would excuse herself after an appropriate interval. If she thought I had remained with the guests too long she would rebuke me afterwards. There were other sources of strain, as well. She grew irritable when I played the piano becuase she did not like music. When I read books in French I would have to translate aloud to her to protect myself from her reproaches. In an effort to improve matters, I invited her to join me in my lessons. She soon tired of French, but kept up an interest in drawing and painting. Indeed she spent long hours at her drawing board and became highly accomplished. Meanwhile, I was able to catch a bit of freedom. My friend stayed with us for five years. All the while we remained like two sisters.

A NEW MENTOR AND HER SALON FOR WOMEN

During that same time, I became acquainted with another woman whom I grew to love and respect. She was the only person who never aroused Atiyya Hanim's jealousy and whom she even conceded deserved my affection. Eugénie Le Brun, a Frenchwoman, was the first wife of Husain Rushdi Pasha. I met her for the first time at a wedding reception and was immediately taken by her dignity, sensitivity and intelligence. In spite of my extreme youth I attracted her attention as well. We were introduced by Rushdi Pasha's sister and spent most of the evening in delightful conversation. Some time later, my brother arranged for me to take a day's excursion on the Nile to the Delta Barrage with Mme Rushdi and a number of other European women. The hours I spent in her company on that occasion were the beginning of a

Portraits of turn of the century Egyptian ladies. Friends of Huda.

close relationship. She soon became a dear friend and valued mentor. She guided my first steps in 'society' and looked out for my reputation.[7]

There had been some gossip about me, Mme Rushdi confided, because I was not living with my husband. It was said that I had left my husband in order to find a younger man. Once after I had left her house at the end of a visit, a European woman who had been there began to talk about Egyptian women, claiming many secrets were hidden behind the veil. She said Egyptian women could camouflage disreputable deeds behind a mask but because the actions of European women were visible their behaviour was the better. Mme Rushdi refuted this, letting her know emphatically that her notions certainly in no way applied to me.

Knowing my interest in Egyptian antiquities, this woman once persuaded me to accompany her to a certain dealer. As we left him, she suggested we stop for tea, but this accorded neither with my preferences nor our customary behaviour. As I was repeatedly refusing she proposed we go to Jazira, a European enclave removed from the centre of town, where I would go unnoticed. I demanded to be taken home at once. She gaped in astonishment.

I also refused the stream of invitations to attend her parties, lavish affairs reflecting her wealth and social status. Suspecting that I was reluctant to accept because both men and women attended – a practice contrary to our customs – she told me that many Muslim women came to her receptions, remaining in a separate room from which they could view the other guests from behind a screen. I reminded her that these women were accompanied by husbands, fathers, or brothers, and that my circumstances were different. Later, I confided in Mme Rushdi, asking her to convey my wishes to be left alone.

Mme Rushdi not only guarded my reputation, but also nourished my mind and spirit. She took it upon herself to direct my reading in French. She would assist me over difficult passages in a book and when I had finished it she would discuss it with me. In that way, she helped me perfect my French and expand my learning.

Soon, at her request, I began to attend her Saturday salon during the hours set aside for women.[8] She would tell me, 'You are the flower of my salon.' On the days when I was unable to attend I used to send flowers. Once she responded with a sweet

The Muski, a large bazaar in an old section of Cairo. Antiquities shops, like the one Huda mentions visiting, were located here. A European woman appears in the background.

note saying that the flowers I had sent could not make up for the absence of her 'beloved flower'. She begged me to lessen the number of bouquets so I would not diminish her joy. Her growing affection toward me made some of her friends jealous but others applauded her devotion to me.

As mistress of the salon, Mme Rushdi adroitly guided the discourse from issue to issue. There were debates about social practices, especially veiling. She confessed that although she admired the dress of Egyptian women, she thought the veil stood in the way of their advancement. It also gave rise to false impressions in the minds of foreigners. They regarded the veil as a convenient mask for immorality. Plenty of lurid tales were circulated by ignorant outsiders about Egyptian morals. Foreigners not infrequently departed from Egypt under the mistaken impression they had visited the houses of respectable families when, in truth, they had fallen into the hands of profiteers who, under the guise of introducing them into the harems of great families, had in fact led them merely to gaudy brothels.

The conversation would move to another topic such as offspring and immorality. Mme Rushdi believed that people who had children never died, as their children were extensions of themselves who kept their memories alive. 'I have no children to perpetuate my memory,' she would say, 'but I shall remain alive through my books.' She once revealed that she had provided for a burial plot in the cemetery of Imam al-Shafai.[9] In answer to our surprised looks she said, 'You didn't know that I embraced Islam after my marriage? I wish to be buried in the Muslim cemetery next to my husband so we shall never be separated in this world or the next.'

Speaking of her books, she said, 'I have signed them, as I have written them – Niya Salima ('In Good Faith'). My purpose in *Harem et les musulmanes* (*The Harem and Muslim women*) was to describe the life of the Egyptian woman, as it really is, to enlighten Europeans. After it appeared in Europe, I received many letters saying my book had cleared up false impressions of life in Islamic countries. They said it had corrected outsiders' images of Egyptians. In fact, they said Egyptians seemed not unlike themselves.' That restored her peace of mind, she said. She had been very upset when she heard that many Egyptians had thought she had criticized the condition of women in Egypt.

'However,' she continued, 'my second book is different. I decided to attack the problem of the backwardness of Egyptian women, demonstrating it arose from the persistence of certain social customs, but not from Islam, as many Europeans believe. Islam, on the contrary, has granted women greater justice than previous religions. While working on the book I attended sessions of the *Shariah* Courts (religious courts where person status or family law cases are heard) to find out for myself how women fared. I was aghast to see the blatant tyranny of men over women. My new book will be called, *Les Repudiées (The Divorcees).*' Mme Rushdi read me portions of the book as she completed them, asking for my reactions.[10]

One day, in private, I asked Mme Rushdi about her marriage. She told me her story.

I married for love. I loved Rushdi very much and respected his fine character. My sister had married a man addicted to alcohol and gambling (I knew Islam forbade both). He squandered her fortune and ruined her life. I was sure Rushdi would never bring me to that end. My father, however, did not approve of the marriage. Fortunately, I had been raised by my grandmother who had encouraged me to think for myself. With support from my sister I was able to persuade my father I would be happy and that Rushdi, coming from a well-to-do family, could provide for me. My father reluctantly consented.

Rushdi was in France at the time, but returned to Egypt suddenly because his father was ill. He promised to come back as soon as possible so we could get married. Some time later he wrote saying that his father had died. Since he had left nothing but debts, and he did not want to place any burdens on me, he told me I should feel free to marry someone else. But he said it would take the joy from his life. When I read that my devotion grew all the more. My family displayed strong reservations, but I became more determined than ever to marry him and won out. My sister asked my father to give me the dowry that was my due. Later she helped me prepare for the trip to Egypt. My sister and a group of friends accompanied my departure.

When I arrived in Alexandria Rushdi was waiting for me. We proceeded to the house of one of his friends where we signed the contract of marriage and then set out for Cairo. At first we moved into the house of his mother on Rudah Island, who treated me well. After falling ill following a miscarriage, I received medical advice to leave Rudah because of the damp Nile air. We rented a house in Bab al-Khalq before moving into our present house in Shariah Yaqub.[11]

I asked Mme Rushdi if she would marry an Egyptian if she had it to do over again. She replied:

> I must confess if I were to relive my life I would not marry into another society because of the constant strain of trying to live according to customs different from those one grew up with. Also, most European women who marry Egyptians are from the lower classes, and it is upsetting when people do not make distinctions. Marriage across cultures is a big mistake.

The period during which Mme Rushdi was working on her book was hectic. Owing to the prominent position of her husband, she was constantly obliged to receive streams of callers petitioning for assistance on all sorts of matters. She expended enormous energy on the endless demands of running a large household. She also sustained a number of shocks related to family and property which affected her heart and weakened her health.

Eventually she left for France. Her health deteriorated further and she was sent to the hospital. From her bed she continued to oversee the remaking of some jewellery for me, writing that she had to have 'a little operation, but please do not worry about me'. She did not survive the operation.

Mme Rushdi died a few months after the death of our national leader, Mustafa Kamil, a good friend of my brother. Qasim Amin, 'The Defender of the Women', followed them the same year (1908). Thus, Egypt lost three valiant strugglers in the service of her cause. Both my brother and my husband, with whom I had recently been reconciled, thanks partly to the efforts of Mme Rushdi, shared my grief for my departed friend.

I had come to rely heavily upon her good counsel but even after her death I felt her spirit light the way before me. When I was about to embark on something, I often paused to ask myself what she would think, and if I sensed her approval I would proceed.

PART FOUR

A WIFE IN THE HAREM

1900–18

RECONCILIATION

Once my brother turned eighteen my mother was eager for him to marry and before long arranged his betrothal to the daughter of Daramalli Pasha. When two years passed and he still had not married I asked him why he was delaying. Finally, Alwi Bey said to me one day, 'Your brother has promised not to marry until you return to your husband. You have been separated seven years now.' I replied that for the sake of my brother I would agree to a reconciliation. The news spread rapidly and was greeted with satisfaction by the family. Later, when my brother thanked me, I told him I was prepared to return to my husband only under certain conditions. I was sure my husband would refuse them, but he did not.

I encouraged my brother to prepare for his wedding. He wanted to dispense with elaborate celebrations and distribute money to the poor instead. I told him to be charitable and have wedding festivities at the same time. He followed my advice, and his wedding was long remembered for its splendour and lavish generosity.

I delayed my return to my husband in the belief I had finally put an end to his demands and would be left in peace. However, I began to see that my continued living apart would be the undoing of my brother, whose wife was growing irritated by his frequent

visits and the affection he lavished upon me. At last, I returned to
my husband.

A CURE IN PARIS

Following the death of Mme Rushdi I became sick with grief and
was advised to go abroad for a cure. My husband and I went to
France. In Paris we stayed near the Champs Elysées in the Princess
Hotel. I marvelled at the bustling Place de la Concorde and was
surprised to find an Egyptian obelisk standing in the centre with
its long, clean lines and handsome hieroglyphs, testimony to the
splendour of ancient Egypt. That awesome monument of civilization symbolized a friendship between Egypt and France that had
been strengthened by ties of history and cultural links. I watched
the fashionably dressed women – men at their sides – promenad-
ing by the graceful fountains which sprayed water in fascinating
shapes. It looked like a festive occasion but I was told it was an
everyday scene.

I liked Paris – not only for its beautiful architecture, gardens and
boulevards, and elegant dress and sophisticated entertainment, but
because there was something to excite the imagination everywhere. Every street and square evoked the deeds of bygone
heroes. Like an open book of the past, the city revealed both the
prosperity enjoyed during the rule of the wise and the privation
endured under the weak. The French flock to palaces, churches
and museums, and historic squares. They grow up familiar with
their past because of the monuments raised to honour those who
have died for the freedom and independence of their country.

I liked the people, even the roughness of the common people,
and admired their individualism in thinking and behaviour. I
believe their intense love of country, for they are French above all,
is the secret of their courage and advancement.

Nevertheless, two things about Paris that I did not like were the
odour of absinthe and cigarette smoke in the cafés, and the smell
of the crowds leaving public places or mingling in the streets. The
pushing crowds dismayed me because I had thought the French
were always courteous. I shall never forget the first time I entered
a shop in Paris during a special sale. Seeing the crowd at the front
door, I paused to let some people enter, out of politeness as we do

Huda wearing hat in Paris.

in the East, thinking someone in turn would allow me to enter. Unfortunately, not a soul was aware even of my existence. Suddenly, I was swept along by the crush of human bodies, pushed and pulled in a churning mass until I was about to cry. When I finally found myself in front of a counter and gently reached for a piece of material, as a lady would do in the East, someone snatched it from my hands. Once again I was on the verge of tears but held them back to avoid ridicule. Finally, using my arms like oars I made my way through the human sea and escaped from the shop. Upon reaching the curb I hailed a taxi. Before I could enter, however, a bystander jumped in without so much as a word of apology.

BEING A MOTHER

After my return to my husband, I was overwhelmed with his consideration and respect. I gave birth to a daughter, Bathna, and a son, Muhammad.

I had begun to settle into a quiet life when my daughter, who had been underweight at birth, became ill in her tenth month. I had been nursing her myself, not wanting to share her with another, but after some time I had no milk. Wet nurses were hard to find.[1] My daughter grew weaker and weaker and finally developed a fever that lasted for months. The doctors differed about her ailment, some suggesting typhoid, others malaria, but all agreed that she needed a change of air. Her father, whose various preoccupations made him reluctant to leave Cairo with her, proposed taking her to his *dahabiyya* anchored on the Nile, where she would enjoy the benefit of the river air.

And so we took her one evening to the *dahabiyya* at Zamalek (a posh quarter of Cairo on Jazira Island).[2] My friend, Atiyya Hanim, accompanying my daughter and her nurse, arrived early. My daughter had already been put to bed when I arrived. I had not yet removed my *izar* and veil when a brilliant flash illuminated the deck. I was about to ask what had happened when my husband, going pale, shouted, 'Get out at once. Throw yourself into the Nile if need be. You can swim.' I rushed inside as he continued to scream 'Get out! Get out!' and grabbed my daughter from her nurse. Holding her tight I rushed toward the exit, making my way down the side of the boat, bending over to protect her from the heat of the flames overhead. I have no idea how I managed to get down the gangplank without falling into the river but I found myself on the bank while Aiyya Hanim and the nurse hurried out behind us.

Masses of people had gathered, making it difficult for us to get through. Among the onlookers were some youths from well-to-do families, who made rude remarks as they jostled us. Some of the bystanders commented to each other that the small bag with the child's belongings must contain our jewels. No one made any attempt to assist us or to go to the *dahabiyya* to see if anyone else was caught inside. When I saw the rich and poor, alike, behaving in this loathsome way I shouted, 'Have you no fear of God? Instead of staring at us and making fun of us you might offer us the shelter of a carriage. What a shame Egypt harbours the likes of you!' I turned to the nurse saying, 'Toss the bag to the crowd. They think it is filled with jewels. Let them scramble after it, leaving a path for our escape.' By then, some of the young men began to apologize and one offered us his carriage. I placed my daughter inside with Atiyya Hanim and the nurse and asked the driver to take them to our house.

At that moment, the *agha* appeared saying the fire was under control. The master, he said, was on the riverbank directing the servants and crew of the houseboat in dowsing the flames. Later we were able to return to the *dahabiyya*, as only the awnings and some of the furniture had been burned. We discovered the fire had been started when a gas lamp overturned.

We were back on the houseboat only two days when another crisis occurred. Late one night, Atiyya Hanim, who had been with my daughter, rushed to me saying, 'Come quickly, the girl's temperature has reached forty-one degrees.' I ran to her room in alarm. She did not respond to my questions and her eyes were glazed. Dampening a sheet with cold water, I removed her clothes and wrapped her up like a mummy. Then I roused my husband and asked him to go at once for the doctor.

A strong wind had meanwhile blown up, swaying the *dahabiyya* to and fro, when suddenly we felt a great thud and feared the boat had been wrecked. A *felucca*, buffeted by the wind, had rammed our side. Meanwhile, my alarm over my daughter continued to mount and I kept insisting that my husband leave at once, but he replied, 'How can we expect the doctor to come all the way here at such an hour, especially when the river is rough?' I said, 'If you won't go, I shall go myself.' When he saw me getting ready to leave, he dressed and left in a *felucca*. I watched him disappear from sight, the sailboat rising and falling in the turbulent waters.

I stayed up all night applying cold packs to my daughter, running to the window every now and then to wait for my husband. At dawn, I began to despair, fearing his *felucca* had capsized and he had drowned. I felt guilty about him and frantic about my daughter. Finally, around eight-thirty he appeared with Dr Hess and Dr Tortolis. When Dr Tortolis saw my daughter he told us to remove her at once from the boat, meanwhile commending me for keeping her bundled in cold sheets. After we returned to the house, the doctors prescribed two injections of phenobarbital.

The following night was frightful. I shall never forget my daughter's fever and how I swung between hope and despair. She woke up at eleven o'clock, frightened and burning as if she were on fire. In her delirium she would have thrown herself out of the bed had we not been there. We remained by her side until morning when Dr Hess arrived. 'Thank God, she is all right,' he said. 'I hardly slept all night. Whenever I heard a sound I thought I was being called.' Dr Hess, may God bless him, was a kindhearted man who had a father's love for the children he brought into the world. He was also merciful and charitable to the poor. In later years, whenever I asked him to visit the poor at home he would respond to the call, day or night. If they could not afford to pay for their medicine he gave it to them for nothing.[3]

Although my daughter recovered from her illness, she remained weak for years. Whenever she contracted an ailment it was usually a severe case. Eventually, the doctors suggested she might benefit from the mountain air in Europe, but her father refused to let her leave Egypt. Finally, when her condition failed to improve, I lost patience and threatened to leave my husband if anything happened to her. Dr Coloradi, our physician in Alexandria, insisted she would not get better without a change of climate, and so my husband granted permission for her to be taken to Turkey.

A TURKISH SUMMER

Accompanied by my mother, I left with my daughter for Stamboul on the SS *Tsaritza*, a small Russian vessel. It was our first voyage abroad by ourselves. The sea was smooth and although I had been unable to sleep well for two months, from the very first night on board I slept peacefully, renewed in my hopes for my daughter's recovery. My mother also relaxed and grew less worried about her own daughter. Bathna's vigour picked up the second day out and she began to run up and down the deck. The passengers, mostly Russian soldiers returning from the war with Japan, showered attention upon her the whole trip.

Having heard all my life how beautiful Turkey was and tales of life there, I was eager to see the country. One day at dusk the ship glided through the Sea of Marmara. Like a bride prolonging the moment of magic, it began its slow approach into the port of Stamboul, at that fleeting moment when the sun's rays fall upon the Golden Horn, illuminating the domes and minarets of mosques around the port. The painted rooftops on the hills dotted the thick woods like roses strewn on a carpet of green. The call to prayer rose through a deep silence bespeaking the majesty of God.

On shore, we hired one of the canopy-covered carriages waiting at the waterside and began our drive up the European side of the Bosporus, toward Buyuk Deree and the *konak* Bashir Agha had rented for us high in the hills, in keeping with the doctor's orders. We bounced along the rough cobblestone road until it became so steep we had to get out and go the rest of the way on foot to the house. Expecting to find every comfort, especially after the arduous ride, I was stunned to see a small wooden house with a tiny courtyard lighted by a single gas lamp. Turning to the *agha*, I asked, 'Weren't you able to find anything better than this? I have been noticing palatial residences all along the shore!' He answered, 'This house was the best I could find and the cleanest, as well.' Had I not been concerned about my mother and daughter who were already exhausted, I would have turned around immediately. As it was, I went upstairs, hoping for something better, but the rooms held only the barest necessities. Deeply disappointed, I resolved to go out at dawn to find more suitable quarters.

But when the sun came up the next morning it revealed one of the most breathtaking sights I had ever seen. The broad expanse of the Bosporus glistened before me, flanked on both sides by high, flower-covered hills with small slant-roofed houses peering out. Below, the elegant residences of foreign embassies looked over the sea, and *yalis* sprawled gracefully to the water's edge. The panorama disarmed my annoyance with the *agha* and prevented me from looking for another house, as did the lovely garden I had just discovered. It was full of flowers and fruit trees. There were cherry trees laden with bright red clusters, and even an apricot tree, like those in my father's garden that had been cut down before my wedding.[4]

While contemplating these sights, I heard a voice say in Turkish, 'My Lady, let us stroll and enjoy the full beauty of this paradise. You need only a *tarha* for your hair and a cloak over your shoulders here on the Bosporus.' Looking up, I recognized Hilmi Pasha's son who used to visit us as a child. I remembered his sister as a gifted and vivacious girl who had mastered Arabic grammar.

Huda in yashmak and ferace – Turkish style veil and cloak.

Hasan, on the other hand, had been fun-loving. When I had last seen him he was still a child. Suddenly, a grown man appeared before me. When I inquired what had brought him to Turkey, he told me that he had qualified as an engineer and was waiting for employment with the Ottoman government. Meanwhile he was assisting Egyptians and other summer visitors in Turkey. Eventually, he was appointed an engineer on the construction of the new railway from Damascus to Madina.

When Hasan assured me I would not find a better place, I began to put the *konak* in order, settling in with my mother and daughter, as well as Mahramat Hanim, a Circassian freedwoman and former slave in the household of Khedive Ismail, who had insisted upon coming along to help. My maid had refused to leave her daughter alone in Egypt.

Mahramat Hanim had been the chief *kalfa* in the palace. On ceremonial occasions, long staff in hand, she used to usher visitors into the presence of the *Walda Pasha* (the khedive's mother and highest ranking in the royal household) and when the presentations were concluded, she would deliver an encomium. She was highly respected and feared by palace servants and slaves – and even some of the princesses – because of her power as head of the royal household female staff and her formidable character.[5] She often called on us at home and became very fond of my daughter. Later when my son, Muhammad, was born we became rivals for her affection. One day in a light moment I said to her, 'I promise, and all here are witness, that if you are still around when my son comes of age, I shall arrange for him to marry you!' I quickly added, 'He can divorce you afterwards if he wishes, of course.' She became furious as we all burst into laughter. While he was growing up, Mahramat Hanim never ceased imploring God to guide him to be an honest and successful man. God called her to him before my son reached manhood.

During our three-months' stay in Turkey, my daughter was treated by a renowned Italian paediatrician, but to no avail. She would improve for a time only to have another, often, worse relapse. More discouraged than ever, I decided we should leave for Egypt, and departed from Turkey, having seen no more than the Bosporus.

While I continued to fight for my daughter's life, everyone around me grew more and more worried about her condition and mine as well. One day, Mme Rushdi (who was alive until the girl reached six) informed me that a specialist in internal medicine, Dr Hobbes, had just arrived from France, and she would bring him to see my daughter. I thanked her somewhat distractedly, owing to my mounting despair. The following day she came with the doctor.

My daughter greeted the doctor with a wan smile. He inquired what diseases she had contracted in the past. When I mentioned a malaria that left her with recurrent fevers, he prescribed a medicine. He announced she was suffering from malnutrition and would die of starvation if her intake of food did not improve. He gave instructions for a more nourishing diet. In time my daughter's health was restored.

I continued to cut myself off from everything else to devote myself entirely to my daughter until that time. Some of my friends started to ignore me, while others, growing impatient, called me 'Umm Bathna', Mother of Bathna, even though I had given birth to a son two and a half years after my daughter's birth. (It was a practice, especially in the popular classes, in Egypt to 'name' a mother in reference to her eldest child but if she had sons to her eldest son.) My husband, too, was becoming irritated because I was not giving him enough attention. I loved my daughter so much I felt I would die of grief if anything happened to her. The love she gave me in return made it even more difficult for me to be away from her for any length of time.

She was an obedient child. I was strict with her, especially about regulating the food she ate. At the same time, I tried to make her understand the reason. If, in my absence, her nurse tried to give her something she shouldn't eat, she would refuse it. When she saw me giving her brother some sweets she would rush to my side holding her mouth up for a kiss. Sometimes, I ate in front of her but she never asked for anything because she knew she mustn't. I was told it was unkind but I did it to encourage discipline and restraint in her, and I believe I succeeded.

I was less successful in my attempts to administer medicines. I recall one day chasing her vainly from room to room, to give her some castor oil. Finally, she reached her brother's room. He tried to help, saying, 'Watch me drink the castor oil!' I thought he was teasing but, suddenly, he opened his mouth and swallowed. I was touched by that – he was only four years old at the time – but he did not succeed either.

In raising my children I tried to apply reason. If they did something wrong I explained what they had done, so they would not repeat it and to help them acquire a sense of right and wrong. I instilled in them a sense of responsibility and uprightness. When I found these traits in them as adults I was reassured I had done the right thing.

THE FIRST 'PUBLIC' LECTURES FOR WOMEN

After my daughter's health improved, I began to see my friends again. The death of my confidante, Mme Rushdi, had forced me to become self-sufficient and not rely on help from others. The year after I lost my dear friend, Marguerite Clement arrived from France on a tour of several eastern countries sponsored by the Carnegie Endowment.[6] After she had said she was interested in meeting Egyptian women, she was introduced to me by a friend, Ali Bey Bahgat.

One evening, as my guest at the Opera House, she talked about her travels and the lectures she gave and asked if Egyptian women were in the habit of giving and attending lectures. We were not, I had to admit, but I invited her to give one. I suggested she compare the lives of oriental women and western women and talk about social practices such as veiling. She asked me to find an older woman to sponsor the event, as I was too young at the time. I was not optimistic about finding anyone. I was certain my mother would not be persuaded to do it. However, that very evening, as we were leaving the box, we met Princess Ain al-Hayat, with whom I had been on cordial terms for a long time. I presented Mlle Clement to her, mentioning the proposed lecture. Would she give her patronage to a general meeting? She accepted without a moment's hesitation.[7]

Next I had to find a suitable place for the talk. My husband suggested a lecture hall at the new university or the offices of the recently founded paper, *al-Jarida*. I preferred the university and requested permission from Alwi Pasha, who proposed holding the lecture on a Friday, when the faculty and students would be in recess. The Egyptian university was, at the time of its foundation, under the patronage of His Highness, Prince Ahmad Fuad, later King Fuad.[8]

The lecture drew a good audience. Mlle Clement had begun to speak when Princess Ain al-Hayat made her entrance. I had reserved chairs in the front row for the princess and her entourage but when they failed to appear after an appropriate interval I ushered some of my relatives into them. As soon as they saw the royal entourage they rose to offer them the chairs. When the others in the audience saw it they stood up as well, whereupon the speaker paused. The princess apologized for the disturbance. Later, I heard that some of the European women present had criticized the episode, remarking that in their countries a speaker would not stop no matter what the status of the latecomer. However, the speaker, herself, was not familiar with our customs. In any case, the lecture was an unprecedented event.

The talk met with such enthusiasm that I invited Mlle Clement to return to give a whole series of lectures for women. His Highness, Prince Ahmad Fuad, supported the women's lectures and ordered a hall to be reserved at the university on Fridays. Soon, Egyptian women began to speak. The best known was

Malak Hifni Nasif who wrote under the name, Bahithat al-Badiyya (Seeker in the Desert).[9]

THE *MABARAT* MUHAMMAD ALI

Shortly after Mlle Clement's lecture, Princess Ain al-Hayat invited me to a tea given for the new Lady Cromer, who wished to thank the women who had supported the dispensary established in memory of the late Lady Cromer.[10] I replied that I had not participated in the work of the dispensary and it was not fitting for me to attend. My mother had supported the charity, however. A few days later, the princess sent for me. When I arrived she received me in bed. 'I understood your reason for not attending the reception for Lady Cromer. It is, indeed, shameful that we in Egypt do not undertake such projects, ourselves. It is our duty to be at the head of charitable works in Egypt. I intend to sponsor a dispensary.' I praised her plan and confessed I had declined to take part in the enterprise headed by an Englishwoman, however much I appreciated the charitable works of Europeans, and notwithstanding the participation of other Egyptian women.

I proposed the establishment of a school, providing classes in infant care, family hygiene, home management, and the like to help spread the benefits of modern health-care. The school could function as an adjunct of the dispensary. The princess promised to give the project serious consideration. However, largely for practical reasons, she decided to concentrate exclusively on the dispensary in the beginning. Before I left she confided, 'I am anxious to encourage the princesses of the royal family and Egyptian women to cooperate in works that will serve the nation and humanity.' She insisted I help her achieve that goal and I pledged my support.

The following week I received an invitation from Princess Ain al-Hayat to come to her palace on Shariah al-Dawawin for the first meeting about the dispensary. Many princesses and Egyptian women attended and, after talk over tea, they elected a committee headed by Princess Nazli Halim, with Princess Ain al-Hayat as treasurer and other princesses as secretaries, as well as Mme Fouquet. We each pledged at least fifty pounds to launch the project. Princess Ain al-Hayat announced that Her Highness, the

Huda in her twenties or early thirties.

Walda Hanim (the mother of Khedive Abbas Hilmi) would make a generous bequest and would give one hundred and twenty pounds each succeeding year, and that Their Highnesses, the Khedive Abbas Hilmi, and the Wife of the Khedive, likewise, would give their support. Princess Ain al-Hayat distributed stamps with the image of a woman embracing a poor girl, to be sold for a piaster each. To increase sales, it was decided to distribute stamps to the various ministries and provincial governorates. The revenue, added to the initial donations, would form the working capital of the society that was to oversee the running of the dispensary.

When summer came, however, Princess Ain al-Hayat went to Europe for medical treatment, and there she died before reaching the age of fifty. I had been very fond of her and admired her intelligence, generosity, and delicate manner. One night, in a dream, she entered my study dressed all in black followed by her daughter, Princess Kazima, who was carrying a closed book placed upon a pillow. I approached the princess to greet her. After returning my greeting, she nodded to her daughter, who gave me the book. I interpreted the dream as a sign that the princess was entrusting me to carry out her plans for the dispensary and I resolved to do everything in my power to fulfil her wishes.

After her death, the other princesses ran into difficulties over the treasury. When they approached her son, Prince Kamal al-Din Husain, about the committee's funds, he asked for the records of their money. But they did not have any receipts for the donations or stamp sales and they began to despair. I suggested that the records of the committee's accounts would surely be found among the late princess's papers. The others said that it would be necessary to search the papers of the late princess's estate, and wished to know who would be competent to examine the accounts once found. I mentioned that a French friend of mine familiar with bookkeeping might assist us, whereupon I was delegated to handle the matter. My friend, the widow of Monsieur Baccus who had taught French at the Taufiqiyya School, volunteered her services. After getting permission from the prince to search, we found the papers and receipts of the committee and proved that its assets amounted to three thousand Egyptian pounds. The prince arranged for prompt payment of the money and thus we were able to move ahead with the dispensary.

We rented a modest building on Shariah Baramuni in the populous Muhammad Ali section of Cairo. We commissioned the architect, Mahmud Pasha Fahmi, to convert the building into a place to house the dispensary and later, a school. Members of the committee took charge of furnishing the new building: Princess Nazli Halim provided forty bolts of white muslin for sheets and bed covers; I donated the beds; my brother gave the desks; and various others took care of additional needs.

On the day of the inauguration ceremonies, Her Highness, the Wife of the Khedive, honoured us by her presence in that small house where Princess Nazli Halim, the head of the committee, and the other members received her. After touring the rooms of the dispensary, she was ushered into the reception hall where the rest of us had gathered. Princess Nazli Halim delivered a short address in Arabic, welcoming Her Highness and thanking her for supporting the new project which she hoped would render worthy services to humanity under the patronage and guidance of His

Highness, the Khedive. The dispensary opened under the name, *Mabarat* Muhammad Ali.

When the work of the *Mabarat* Muhammad Ali expanded I was honoured to become head of the new executive committee. Princess Nazli Halim, head of the original committee was a member along with Princesses Sivekiar, Aziza Hasan, Bahiga Tusun, Zina Hasan and Irfat Hasan; the Egyptian women included *Haram* Takla Pasha, *Haram* Rushdi Pasha, and *Haram* Shafiq Pasha. A Frenchwoman, Mme Carleton de Fière, served as treasurer. The dispensary was administered by an Irish woman, Miss Crouser, a specialist in childcare, who was assisted by a number of Egyptian women. Several Egyptian and European doctors volunteered their services, including Alwi Bey, Sayyid Bey Rifaat, Sami Kamil, Abd al-Hamid Waafa, and Rodier, a French ear, nose, and throat specialist. Sayyida Tumshush assisted with eye examinations. We later requested His Highness, the Khedive, to confer the title of Pasha on Alwi Bey and to decorate Dr Rodier for his services. The operations of the *Mabarat* Muhammad Ali were supervised by the women of the executive committee, who took turns at the headquarters. The valuable humanitarian services of the *Mabarat* continue to this day.

To raise money, the committee of the *Mabarat* Muhammad Ali began holding annual charity fêtes in royal and aristocratic palaces, of a splendour that evoked the days of Harun al-Rashid (the famous Abbassid Caliph of Baghdad). I remember the very first one, at Prince Umar Tusun's palace in Shubra, the likes of which Egypt had not seen since the days of Khedive Ismail. The princesses and princes, rivalling each other to make it a success, sent their most precious possessions for display. The khedive loaned his enormous collection of antique, jewel-encrusted arms. Prince Tusun exhibited a priceless set of Saxe china, a gift of King Louis Philippe of France, and my brother Umar loaned some Pharaonic antiquities that still remain in the house of our late father.

Rooms in the Tusun Palace were transformed to mirror the motif of the extravaganza, the *zifaf*, wedding celebrations of old, as known in the palaces of rulers and princes. A bridal chamber was fitted out with gilded furniture inset with diamonds, pearls and other precious gems. In the banquet hall, a gigantic tray of solid gold stood at the centre of the room, in the ancient manner, upon which were placed golden spoons inlaid with pearls and coral, and a magnificent golden ewer and basin. Surrounding tables held an immense collection of gold plate embellished with diamonds, emeralds and rubies. The great hall where the principal entertainments were held was ornamented with masses of trees and shrubs festooned with coloured lamps. At the centre of the hall stood a *mashrabiyya* cage with cashmere shawls swagged round the wooden grille. It was amusing to see the singers and musicians being ushered blindfolded by eunuchs into the cage to prevent them from seeing the women. Scattered around the enclosure were heaps of cushions for the women to sit upon while they enjoyed the music and singing of Egyptian and Turkish performers, including Shaikh Yusif al-Minyawi, much acclaimed in Egypt at the time.

Everyone was splendidly attired. Princesses, decked out in heirloom jewels, appeared in gowns their grandmothers had worn, while young girls stood nearby fanning them with ostrich and peacock feathers studded with precious stones. The Egyptian women also dressed in the sumptuous styles of old. Among the special guests were the wife of the heir to the German throne and princesses of the British royal family. His Highness, the Khedive, honoured the large gathering of royalty and aristocracy with his presence. There was no mingling of women and men, but a special place was set aside for the men, many of whom paid hundreds of pounds for a brief glimpse of the festivities in the main rooms.

In the years to come, the Zaafaran Palace and others were the scenes of receptions no less magnificent. In this way we raised substantial sums for the work of the *Mabarat* Muhammad Ali.

THE INTELLECTUAL ASSOCIATION OF EGYPTIAN WOMEN

The intellectual awakening of upper-class women that had been underway over the past years, stimulated and shaped in part by the women's salon and the lecture series, convinced me of the need for an association to bring women together for further intellectual, social and recreational pursuits. I mentioned the idea to some of the princesses and asked for support, which they willingly agreed

Huda at home in Cairo.

to give. We met in my house to conclude plans. Princess Amina Halim presided over the gathering of princesses, Egyptians and foreign women. Thus in April 1914 the Intellectual Association of Egyptian Women was born. Among the members were Mai Ziyada, the gifted writer, then at the beginning of her literary career, and Labiba Hashim, the founder and editor of the magazine, *Fatat al-Sharq* (*The Young Woman of the East*, established in 1906), who also served as the Arabic secretary.

In my correspondence with Marguerite Clement, continuing since her visit to Egypt, I had revealed my hopes for creating an intellectual society for women. She promised, if it happened, she would come to Egypt to take part in our programme and offered to give lectures on themes of our choice. I wrote a formal request for her to present to officials in France to facilitate her travel. She came to Cairo and delivered a series of lectures held in my house and at the Egyptian university. She also became a corresponding member of the society.

Before long, I began to search for a headquarters for our society which we had dared not call a club (*nadi*), as our traditions would not allow it. At that time it was still not acceptable for women to have a place of their own outside private houses. With the approach of summer many of the princesses departed for Europe, as usual. They expected the final arrangements for the headquarters to be made by the time they returned.

THE FINAL ILLNESS OF NIECE HUDA

At about this time, Huda, the daughter of my brother, became very ill. My brother and I, who loved her dearly, used to say in her presence that she would be the bride of my son, Muhammad. The idea was taken up by the children, who grew to be very fond of each other. When they played, if Muhammad happened to hit Huda she would never rebuke him. If asked how she could marry such a cruel boy she would say that it was no one's business and that she would marry him no matter what. To the suggestion that he might marry someone else she would answer that it would not prevent her from marrying him as well. Muhammad shared her feelings. One day, when I said to him, 'Do you think she will wait for you? She is a year older than you and girls usually marry earlier than boys,' he began to cry and asked me, 'Who shall I marry then?' He asked that question as if there was no one in the world but her.

In her illness Huda suffered great pain despite all the efforts of her father to see that she had the best care. A physician from Paris, Professor Rubin, attended her, and medicines were sent to Egypt by special mail, all in vain. As death approached, she entrusted her *dada* to take care of her little dog and said she could hear the sounds of birds singing in the garden. 'What a beautiful sound, what a beautiful garden. I think it is paradise.' She died immediately after uttering those words, as if she had been born for that paradise which her soul entered before it departed the earth.

The death profoundly affected her father, and we were all shocked, including my son, Muhammad who was plunged into grief, despite his tender age. At that time he, too, had not been well and was plagued by fevers. When the doctors could not determine the cause they advised me to take him to specialists in

Europe and to seek the mountain air. I was forced to travel abroad.

A EUROPEAN SUMMER ON THE EVE OF WAR

I had to leave my mother behind, sick in bed, because the doctor forbade her to travel, although he assured us that she would be all right so long as she didn't suffer any emotional shocks. I set out burdened with sadness and worry, grieving for the death of my brother's daughter and anxious for the health of my mother and son. I had never travelled before without the company of my mother. I had the feeling I would never see her again and was about to turn back when I reach Alexandria, but my son's condition prevented me from doing so. We departed – the Pasha, my brother, his wife, and our children.

In Paris my son was examined by doctors who advised a cure in the mountains. As my husband was in need of treatments at the mineral springs in Vittel, we decided to go there and afterwards to the mountains. Hasan, his son, a student in England, was on holiday at the time and would join us.

While we were in Paris I was invited to attend a large meeting for women who were agitating for peace and the right to vote. The meeting took place in a huge hall belonging to one of the French newspapers. Many women made speeches including Mme Sévigné, Avril de St Croix, and my friend, Marguerite Clement.[11] I observed women, the youth and even some military officers, enthusiastically advocating peace. I was impressed. I began to think that Europeans had reached a high stage of advancement, but was soon disabused of that idea. On the following day, I attended a lecture on psychological illnesses given by the well-known professor, Père Villon, the brother of a friend of mine. When I congratulated him on the talk, he said he had heard I had attended the peace meeting the day before. 'Are you a supporter of peace?' I said, 'Yes.' 'How can that be when you are an Egyptian and your country is occupied by the British army?' I replied, 'I believe in the victory of justice over force.' 'Will the British leave your country peacefully? Would it be in their own interests to do so? Mlle Clement must have influenced you,' he said, 'I am among Frenchmen who await the day we can return the insult of the

Germans.' I said I was sorry to hear him speak like that, especially after having witnessed the spirit of harmony between French and Germans at the meeting. I expressed the hope that he would change his mind. He answered, 'I hope you will come around to my way of thinking.'

While the Pasha was concluding his treatment at Vittel, I did some shopping in Paris. The hotels were filled up with summer visitors and had no room for Hasan and me. So, we stayed with my maid, Margaret, at a flat belonging to my brother. I was surprised to find the streets of Paris quiet, the cafés closed at night and faces sad and uneasy. I heard talk of the possibility of war between France and Germany which I refused to believe. Europe seemed too civilized and enlightened to resort to war, the most brutal act imaginable. When my friend, Margucrite Clement, visited me, her face was pale and she was bent as if carrying a heavy burden. She said that the international situation was grave and war was likely. When I asked what she and her colleagues in the peace movement would do, she said, 'We will stand by our people. But, our voice is still weak.' Despite these grim words I could not believe war would come.

The train back to Vittel was uncharacteristically empty. The Pasha and children who were waiting anxiously for us at the station said that the hotel was empty and that the local inhabitants were leaving the town because it was close to the border and they feared hostilities between the French and Germans. That was on 29 July. The hotel employees were sad, especially the maids, because their husbands had been called up. The manager, preparing to deliver sacks of money to the bank, said he was ordered to close the hotel. My husband asked him to change fifty French pounds and the manager, silent for a moment, replied, 'At your service, even though this is not allowed.'

We left Vittel for Switzerland the first of August. We were supposed to change trains a few hours later for one with a dining car, but the second train did not appear. When it grew late we asked the station master what had happened and he answered brusquely, 'Is this a time for touring, especially with children?' We did not know till that moment that it was mobilization day. Trains moved past filled with soldiers waving flags and singing patriotic songs while women with tears in their eyes were bidding them farewell. Later we were able to board another train for Switzerland.

As soon as we arrived in Basle we headed for the nearest hotel, but the manager said he had no vacancies. I asked him if he thought I was about to take my young children and go out into the streets at three o'clock in the morning looking for a place. When I suggested that we sleep on the couches in the lounge, which he said was forbidden, he procured rooms for us by telephone at a hotel in the old city on the other side of the Rhône and ordered taxis to take us there. It was a small, simple hotel but very clean. The maid brought us milk, cheese and bread and before long we went to sleep. The next morning we saw golden-haired and blue-eyed boys and girls, playing in the street. Their gaiety lifted my fatigue and some of the melancholy that had filled me after seeing the tearful women bid their men off to war. However, even the children filled me with anguish as I thought of the young ones who would be orphaned by war.

From Basle we went to Zurich, where the train station was also filled with soldiers and their relatives, while a band played military music. Our hotel there was so crowded we had to sleep in the reception room and take breakfast in the dining hall.

Zurich, splendidly laid out along an exquisite lake, was one of the most beautiful cities I had ever seen. On a walk with the children I found a funicular that went to a place on the outskirts called Zurichburg. There I found a lovely hotel, and we took rooms in it on the following day. We were sorry we did not speak German and sometimes had difficulty making ourselves under-stood. One day, as I walked with the children in the wooded area near the hotel, a man passing by said a few words I could not understand. I was taken aback that he would speak to people he had never met. A little while later another man on a horse with an old-fashioned saddle called out a few words of German, and again I was surprised. Afterwards I learned that it is a Swiss custom to greet people on the road, especially on country lanes. That was exactly the habit of the Egyptian *fallah*.

The Pasha decided that we should leave Switzerland and return to Egypt via Italy. The train to Milan was so crowded that we were obliged to occupy a third-class carriage even though we had first-class tickets. In Milan we stayed at a small hotel in order to economize. Our finances had begun to dwindle, especially after we had encountered a number of Egyptians who asked for help after their money had run out. Sympathetic to their plight, the

Pasha gave them most of what he had, and the banks would not cash more than twenty francs a day. Our uncomfortable hotel overlooked the Piazza del Duomo which was so crowded and noisy, mainly from the cries of newspaper vendors, that we could not rest day or night. We stayed in Milan only briefly, before departing for Genoa to take a ship back to Egypt.

All ships were fully booked at that time, but we managed to get reservations from an Egyptian who had arranged passage on an Italian ship. I wanted to return to Egypt as fast as possible so that my sick mother would not grow anxious over us when she learned that war had broken out. A shock might bring her closer to the grave. The SS *Oriente* departed on 10 August around midnight. Our staterooms were uninhabitable, owing to the dirt and excessive heat, and no other rooms were available. When some of the ship's officers offered their cabins at a stiff price the Pasha gave them nearly all his money to secure our comfort. Relieved, we went upstairs and found the rooms well ventilated. But, no sooner had we put our heads on our pillows than we were attacked by swarms of cockroaches. We bundled the children out of the room and spent the night in chairs on the deck. The next morning we requested the captain to have a tent set up on the deck so we could sleep there. The Pasha slept in a chair next to Muhammad, while I, scarcely able to sleep for fear one of the children would fall to the deck, occupied one next to my daughter. One night, as my weary eyes began to close, I heard what I thought was the sound of a body hitting the deck, and awoke screaming. Bathna had rolled over and I could hear her saying, 'Mama, don't be afraid. Nothing has happened to me.'

On the fourth day out we steamed slowly towards Naples in a dense fog, the ship's horn blowing frightening blasts. Suddenly, there was a large jolt followed by screaming from the direction of the third class. Fearing that our ship had collided with another, I ran to the railing and looked down at the sea. Hats and pieces of wood were floating on the water. I began to run in search of my children so they would be near me if we sank. Meanwhile, the captain announced that we had hit a fishing boat and that the fishermen were in the water. Officers and crew members from our ship were lowered in boats to pick up the fishermen. The sailors, dressed in white, standing erect in the boats with foghorns at their mouths, looked like phantoms in the eerie mist. For two hours they searched for the last fisherman, but he was never found. The rescue boats returned and the fog lifted as if it had never existed. It was one of those fateful moments when the angel of death snatches up those chosen by destiny. The crew asked for donations from the passengers for the families, but pockets were empty and only about ten pounds were collected. That evening, the ship entered the port of Naples where it stayed loading potatoes all night. We were unable to sleep after the shock.

The next day, the ship arrived at Catania. We saw women on the beach in their national dress, which resembled oriental clothes. They wore long, black skirts fringed with lace or a swathe of coloured material and covered their heads with black shawls pinned up at the back, reminiscent of the old-fashioned *izar*. The ship was to stay in port all day, so we explored that fascinating town where the Arabs had once been and where there are remnants of their monuments and their customs. We visited a number of churches, as well. It happened to be a saint's day, the feast of a woman saint. We watched a religious procession led by a priest in a purple robe; some people were kneeling at either side of the road while others rushed forward to kiss the hem of his robe. We were astonished at the depth of their religious feeling. Afterwards, we bought the few things we were able to pay for and hurried to the ship. I was relieved when the ship pulled out because we feared that if Italy declared war we would be forced to remain. We were sure our worst fears had been realized when we saw a small boat coming after us to guide the ship back to port, but the captain, informed of our apprehensions, said jokingly that the ship had a huge supply of potatoes that would last a good long time. I feared that the delay would be the death of my mother.

I saw other women weeping, like myself, at the unexpected delay. Their money had run out and they were worried about how they would earn a living during the war, for most of them had no profession. As for our livelihood, I had enough jewellery and precious stones to maintain my children and myself for years. One said, 'I am a good cook and if I am detained in Italy I can work as a chef in a pension or with a family.' Another said, 'I cannot sew or cook so what shall I do?' After a pause she continued, 'Maybe I could be a nanny.' When I heard that I asked myself what I would do in their position. I could neither cook nor sew nor leave my children to work in someone's home. It was a lesson for me and afterwards I learned how to cook and sew. In later years, I admired the courage and ingenuity of the Russian women I met in Egypt after the war, some of whom were princesses but they were not ashamed to earn honourable livelihoods after migrating from their country. One of them, whose flair for needlework I admired, told me she found consolation and satisfaction in producing work that people appreciated. She confessed she had not fully understood the meaning of life until she had begun to be creative and take on responsibilities.

After the ship anchored again at Catania we learned that the steamship company had requested that the ship be re-coaled in Alexandria. When they found it would be impossible, the ship had to turn around to take on coal for the return voyage. Our departure was delayed for another twenty-four hours, but we were greatly relieved that Italy had still not entered the war.

TWO DEATHS

We docked in Alexandria on 19 August, surprised to find no one waiting for us except a clerk and a young woman who was the Arabic teacher of my daughter. I was in a hurry to see my mother and to know that she was well. We left the nanny and our servant in the customs shed to finish the proceedings while we headed immediately for Ramleh. There a messenger handed me a telegram. With trembling hands I opened the envelope and read that my mother had died.

I cannot convey the impact of that terrible moment which will never leave my memory. How fate mocks us. How cruel fate is. When I left Europe I thought of the meeting that would draw near. The very hour my feet touched the soil of my country, as I was telling myself that I was about to see my mother to comfort her and bring joy to her sad soul, she departed this life. Her kind heart was in pain over our separation and she worried for our lives. I was told when she could no longer speak, she would move her eyes from the clock to the door, and the door to the clock, dreading her time would come, that she would leave this world without seeing her two children again and knowing they were safe. Atiyya Hanim who remained at her side during our absence had sent a fake telegram to her before our arrival announcing we had landed in Alexandria.

Leaving my two children in the care of their *dada* and the teacher who had come to meet us, I set out immediately with my husband for Cairo on the three o'clock train. I spent that night weeping next to the bed of my mother. We transported her body to Minya in Upper Egypt, and crossed the Nile to the tombs in Sharq where she had prepared a final resting place for herself next to my father. The following day, I returned to Cairo.

I grieved deeply at my loss of this dear woman toward whom I felt both the love of a daughter and the love of a mother. These two feelings commingled during the time I cared for her in her long illness. At the end, I felt like an orphan and a bereaved mother at the same time. It was a strange anguished feeling that rent me and I thought it was the greatest sorrow I would ever experience. I never imagined fate was harbouring a blow still more cruel, the death of my dear brother and my only support. I bore that blow as I have borne others. Yet, I thanked God for taking my mother to His side before my brother. My brother tried to compensate for what I lost, as if he had a premonition I would soon be deprived of him, as well. For three years he showered love and affection upon me.

The First World War brought great political upheaval in Egypt. Khedive Abbas Hilmi was deposed and Sultan Husain ascended to the throne. I remember Sultan Husain visiting the Pasha to discuss what the British had offered him and if he should accept to rule and on what basis.

My brother used to visit me every day, if not in the morning then in the evening. We discussed war and politics. I admired the Allies. However, he called them imperialists and blamed them for starting the war. He hoped for victory for the Turks and Germans. Later we discovered how correct his views on imperialism were.

One night a frightening dream made me cry in my sleep and gasp for breath. When my husband woke me up and asked what was wrong, I told him about the dream. I had gone to Minya, to the house of my brother who was there at the time. I found my mother sweeping the floor in front of his room, looking sad and mournful. I asked her about my brother and his wife and she told me they were separated from each other, whereupon I went out to look for them. I entered the room next to the front door and saw my brother's wife dressed in black. At her side was her sister, the wife of Husain Bey Riyad, also wearing a black *izar*. They were about to depart angrily. I tried to stop them and to talk to them but they only looked at me scornfully. I felt hurt and cried. That dream left me with gloomy forebodings but I never thought it had anything to do with my brother.

The following morning, when my brother arrived from Upper Egypt, he asked me why I had not taken up his invitation to come to Minya with my friends to spend a few days with him. Despite my excuses he insisted that I should come as soon as possible. That was Saturday, 15 February 1917, and I promised him I would go the following Tuesday. However, the illness of my friend, Wagida Khulusi,[12] prevented me from leaving that day, and during the night my son came down with a severe fever.

On Wednesday morning my husband awakened me early, the same way he had on the night of my dream. I was upset and asked what had happened to my son. He said, 'I aroused you so we can proceed to Minya because your sister is very ill.' I replied, 'How

Huda's brother Umar with nationalist leader Mustafa Kamil. The two men were friends, and Umar gave financial backing to Kamil's nationalist work.

can I leave with my son sick in bed?' He answered, 'She is on her deathbed,' and a moment later said, 'She has died.' These words made me very sad but my thoughts were fixed on my son whose body was ablaze with fever. 'My sister is dead and does not need me but my son is ill and needs me. I still do not know what is wrong because the doctor has not come yet.' He insisted, 'You must go. You do not want to be criticized.' I went to my son's room to see how he was and gave his *dada* a series of instructions. Putting on my *izar* I left the house mourning my sister and worrying about my son at the same time.

We were greeted at the Cairo train station by Sayyid Agha, whose face showed signs of sadness. After boarding the train my husband left me, according to custom, and proceeded to the section where the men were seated. Sayyid Agha remained with me. When I told him about my dream he said, 'Your dream has come true.' I said, 'Have he and his wife quarrelled and separated? If that has happened my return to my son will be delayed.' He did not answer. While we travelled I imagined my brother waiting for me at the station, as he usually did, and of his grief over the death of our sister. Her sons, Muhammad Ibrahim and Fuad Sultan, were raised in our family house at Minya. My brother used to call Fuad his son. He had drunk the milk of Fuad's mother and it was he who had named him Fuad Sultan. This sister was the second daughter of my father, by his marriage to the daughter of his father's brother. She had loved my mother, who was the same age, and my mother reciprocated that affection.

When the train pulled into the Minya station I did not see my brother waiting for me but found instead one of our half-brothers. My brother, I assumed, was receiving people who had come to pay their condolences. When I inquired if we should go to Bani Ahmad, our sister's village, or to the house of my brother, our half-brother replied, 'Of course, to his house.' It then occurred to me that our sister had died at my brother's house, where she must have gone to visit and to wait for me to come from Cairo.

As we passed through town, I was surprised by the extreme sorrow written on the faces of everyone in the streets and I noticed that all the shops were closed. I was amazed at sounds of screaming and crying from women in the streets and houses. I asked myself, 'Was our sister so deeply loved? Did her kindness touch all these souls?'

At the house people were crowded in between the front gate and the door, crying and yelling as if on judgement day. I was barely able to get through even though people were trying to make way for me. The bystanders regarded me with a frozen expression. Later, I heard they thought I had lost my mind under the impact of severe shock. I was not crying, and they could only see signs of bewilderment on my face. When I reached the main hall, the wife of my brother met me with the words, 'You see what has befallen us?' I said, 'Did my sister die here in this house?' She said, 'Our loss is your brother.'

I felt as if she had driven a dagger into my heart. I went numb and the next thing I knew I was being lifted off the floor. My mouth opened with screams. It was as if I were letting out a fire raging inside me. Next it came to me that my brother might still be alive and had only fainted. I rushed to his room where he lay peacefully with a beautiful smile on his lips. Not noticing the pallor of death on his face, I threw myself on him, kissing him and calling his name. I asked his servant who was standing by the bed to help me massage his body, especially his feet which were colder than the rest of his limbs. My sudden hope and the efforts I had expended in massaging his body helped bring me to my senses. I talked to him. But he never answered me.

My husband entered the room with some of my relatives and asked me to leave so my brother's body could be prepared for burial. Clinging to the bed, I pleaded, 'Leave me with my brother. Do not rush to bury him. He may awaken from his sleep. Don't you see how his face still has the freshness of life?' When I realized they were about to carry me out, I asked my husband to have the tomb of my brother left open and guarded during the night because I was certain he would awaken from his deep sleep. My husband agreed. I left the room with the hope that the ablutions would rouse my brother from his sleep.

He was buried in the tomb next to my father. We spent the whole night there. It was the blackest night of our lives. The following day we returned from the burial grounds across the river.

When my brother departed my interest in life departed with him. We had shared great intimacy. He had been the joy of my life and a source of communication and consideration. With his passing I felt I had lost a link between myself and the world. If it were not for my children I would not have lived a single moment after my brother's death.

The son I had left behind came down with measles. As soon as he recovered my husband ordered him and his sister to be brought to Upper Egypt to be near the children of their late uncle. In the days to come, I spent long hours reading to my children and the children of my dead brother, scarcely aware of what I read. It soothed the children and it soothed me at the same time. Yet, despite the consolation and solace I found in comforting the children, I grew weak. I was ill for five months. My pain over the loss of my brother got worse. I missed his kindness. I had never known such kindness from anyone else. I despaired of recovery. However, the doctors treating me understood my shock.

THE BRIDGE OF NATIONALISM

I was finally on the path to recovery and my strength had begun to return when another experience caused me to feel, acutely, the loss of my brother.

One day my husband spoke with me about requesting the hand of Naila, the daughter of my late brother, for his son, Hasan. Naila was no more than fourteen. Hasan was no more than twenty. He had not completed his education and lacked qualifications. Concerned for the future of my niece, I spoke frankly with my husband asking him not to be hasty. He became angry and accused me of being an obstacle to the marriage. His manner towards me changed just at a time when I was in need of someone to lighten my burdens following the death of my brother. Only my children were able to help me bear the bitterness of life.

Hasan took advantage of the situation. He tried to increase the strain between his father and me. He began interfering in the running of the household and became aggressive towards the servants for no reason, especially the ones most loyal to me. He did many more things I don't care to mention.

I would have separated from my husband because of Hasan, if it had not been for the nationalist movement. My attention was drawn from my private life to serving my country. The Egyptian national movement brought my husband and me closer to each other.

EPILOGUE

The final years in Huda's memoirs, from 1919 to 1924, were highly charged. Both women and men fought for national liberation. It was up to women to initiate the fight for their own liberation. This epilogue tells the story of women's dual struggle as reflected in Huda's memoirs.

Huda and other upper-class women had been living through a period of change and confrontation, as her account reveals, themselves still hidden by the discretion and distancing harem convention required. When the Egyptian nation under imperialist oppression rose up to take matters into its own hands, the only way to achieve independence, all Egyptians participated. Upper-class women ignored harem convention, and so did men, in the fight for national liberation. Women's unprecedented acts were welcomed and justified by national needs.

Egyptians demanded independence at the end of the First World War. In 1919, after they had been denied the chance to discuss their demands in London, they formed the Wafd to voice their demands on home soil. They no sooner did this under the leadership of Saad Zaghlul than the British arrested him and other Wafdist leaders and deported them to the Seychelles. Huda's husband, the treasurer of the Wafd, was not among those deported, and was left in charge. The next day, March 9th, the first of many demonstrations broke out in Cairo and soon spread to other cities and towns throughout the country. All classes rose up. Huda and other upper-class women – anywhere from one hundred and fifty to three hundred according to witnesses – poured out of their harems, clad in veils, on to the streets to demonstrate.[1]

Huda has vivid recall of this historic moment.[2]

> We women held our first demonstration on 16 March to protest the repressive acts and intimidation practised by the British authority. In compliance with the orders of the authority we announced our plans to demonstrate in advance but were refused permission. We

began to telephone this news to each other, only to read in *al-Muqattam* that the demonstration had received official sanction. We got on the telephone again, telling as many women as possible that we would proceed according to schedule the following morning. Had we been able to contact more than a limited number of women, virtually all the women of Cairo would have taken part in the demonstration.

On the morning of 16 March, I sent placards to the house of the wife of Ahmad Bey Abu Usbaa, bearing slogans in Arabic and French painted in white on a background of black – the colour of mourning. Some of the slogans read, 'Long Live the Supporters of Justice and Freedom', others said 'Down with Oppressors and Tyrants' and 'Down with Occupation'.

We assembled according to plan at the Garden City Park, where we left our carriages. Having agreed upon our route and carefully instructed the young women assigned to carry the flags and placards in front, we set out in columns towards the legation of the United States and intended to proceed from there to the legations of Italy and France. However, when we reached Qasr al-Aini Street, I observed that the young women in front were deviating from the original plan and had begun to head in the direction of *Bait al-Umma* (The House of the Nation), as Saad Zaghlul's house was called. I asked my friend Wagida Khulusi[3] to find out why we were going toward Saad Pasha's house and she returned saying that the women had decided it was a better route. According to our first plan we were to have ended our demonstration there. Reluctantly I went along with this change. No sooner were we approaching Zaghlul's house than British troops surrounded us. They blocked the streets with machine guns, forcing us to stop along with the students who had formed columns on both sides of us.

I was determined the demonstration should resume. When I advanced, a British soldier stepped toward me pointing his gun, but I made my way past him. As one of the women tried to pull me back, I shouted in a loud voice, 'Let me die so Egypt shall have an Edith Cavell' (an English nurse shot and killed by the Germans during the First World War, who became an instant martyr). Continuing in the direction of the soldiers, I called upon the women to follow. A pair of arms grabbed me and the voice of Regina Khayyat[4] rang in my ears. 'This is madness. Do you want to risk the lives of the students? It will happen if the British raise a hand

Saad Zaghlul Pasha, National Leader.

against you.' At the thought of our unarmed sons doing battle against the weaponry of British troops, and of the Egyptian losses sure to occur, I came to my senses and stopped still. We stood still for three hours while the sun blazed down on us. The students meanwhile continued to encourage us, saying that the heat of the day would soon abate. Some of the students departed for the legations of the United States, France, and Italy, announcing that the British had surrounded the women in front of Saad Pasha's house. I did not care if I suffered sunstroke – the blame would fall upon the tyrannical British authority – but we stood up to the heat and suffered no harm. The British also brought out Egyptian soldiers armed with sticks.

What these troops were commanded to do is recounted by the man who gave them their orders, the British commandant of the Cairo police, Russell Pasha. 'At a given signal I closed the cordon and the ladies found their way opposed by a formidable line of Egyptian conscript police who had been previously warned that they were not to use violence but to stand still . . . considerable

A school girl, surrounded by other students, on the balcony of 'The House of the Nation', Saad Zaghlul's house, during the revolution, encourages the crowds below.

licence was given them by their officers to practise their ready peasant wit on the smart ladies who confronted them.'[5]

When the men began to taunt their compatriots as Huda tells it,

The women rebuked the soldiers. Some were moved to the point of tears. Eventually Russell Pasha arrived. 'You have conducted your demonstration in defiance of orders. Now that you have done what you set out to do you are requested to return home.' I answered, 'We read in *al-Muqattam* yesterday that the authorities had granted permission for the demonstration. Why do you now stand in our way?' He replied that permission had not been granted and the news was false. Yielding in the face of force, we made our way to our carriages. After departing from the scene we called on some of the foreign legations to inform them of events and to register protest against the Protectorate (imposed by the British in 1914) and martial law. We received courtesy but nothing more. Before returning home we promised to hold another demonstration.[6]

Russell Pasha, in a letter to his father, described the women's demonstration in a condescending tone. 'My next problem was a demonstration by the native ladies of Cairo. This rather frightened me as if it came to pass it was bound to collect a big crowd and my orders were to stop it. Stopping a procession means force and any force you use on women puts you in the wrong. Well, they assembled in motor cars, etc. got out and started to walk in a procession ... I let them get a little way and then blocked them in with police supported by troops and there the dear things had to remain for an hour and a half in the hot sun with nothing to sit on except the curb stone.'[7]

The nationalist movement brought husbands and wives who normally led more separate existences in the divided harem world into closer contact as Huda's memoirs indicate. She tells us that this was the moment of greatest collaboration between herself and her husband. At a time when streets were full of angry demonstrators and armed troops and there were constant arrests and deportations, women had thrown themselves into the movement, and men needed their help. Huda says, 'My husband kept me informed of events so that I could fill the vacuum if he were imprisoned or exiled.'

Women's demonstration in Cairo during 1919 National Revolution.

Women sewed crescents and crosses on green cloth to proclaim the solidarity of Muslims and Christians.

Huda, who up to then had lived a life removed from national politics, threw herself into political activism. Following a demonstration in which some Egyptians were shot she wrote her first letter of protest to Lady Brunyate, an American by birth and long-time friend, the wife of Sir William Brunyate, the judicial and financial adviser to the Egyptian government.

> During these sad times I should like to remind you of the conversations we had last summer at my house in Ramleh. You assured me that Britain had taken part in the war to do service to the cause of justice and humanity, to protect the freedom of oppressed peoples and safeguard their rights. Would you kindly tell me if you remain convinced of this today? May I ask what you think when your government accords itself the right to impose martial law in time of peace and banishes people from their own land when they ask for nothing but the right to live in freedom in their own country and to be hospitable to all?

Before sending the letter, Huda showed it to her husband. He, in turn, showed it to the Wafd, who applauded it. The letter was never answered. Huda says, 'I thought she might have some influence and at the very least I expected her to answer my letter. Instead, she broadcast her dismay to our mutual friends and acquaintances.'

In April, Saad Zaghlul and his companions were released from detention by the British and the Wafd was allowed to go abroad for negotiations. The next day, Huda and women of different classes formed part of a huge demonstration headed by cabinet ministers including members of the Legislative Assembly, army officers, religious scholars, judges, lawyers, doctors, government employees and workers and students. 'Upper-class women rode in carriages and women of the lower class rode in carts. As the women's carriages passed in front of one of the large hotels some soldiers tried to grab an Egyptian flag from the hand of the wife of Ratib Pasha and in the process struck her arm. Unable to get the flag, they hit her carriage with their bayonets. Foreigners cheered her from the hotel terrace.'

The uprising continued,

> The women continued to support the Wafd and at the same time gave encouragement to the people. We consoled relatives of students and others injured by British bullets, visited the wounded, and did what we could to assist the poor and needy among them. In the working class quarters women went to their windows and balconies to applaud their men in displays of national solidarity. Sometimes soldiers fired at the houses, killing and wounding women. Some were hit by bullets that pierced the walls of their houses. The death of Shafiqa bint Muhammad, the first woman killed by a British bullet, caused widespread grief. Egyptians of all classes followed her funeral procession. It became the focus of intense national mourning.[8] Events like these, coming one after the other, did not please the British. They disregarded the solemnity of funeral processions, often scattering the mourners and precipitating bloody confrontations. We women began to compile a list of the dead and wounded. Among the women I remember Shafiqa bint Muhammad, Aisha bint Umar, Fahima Riyad, Hamida bint Khalil, and Najiyya Said Ismail – all from the working classes.

Not only did women of all classes rise up together but women of different religions worked closely together. Huda remarks on the solidarity of the various religions in Egypt which would not allow the colonial power to ignite sectarian strife. She says, 'The British claimed our national movement was a revolt of the Muslim majority against religious minorities. This slander aroused the anger of the Copts and other religious groups. Egyptians showed their solidarity by meeting together in mosques, churches, and synagogues. *Shaikhs* walked arm in arm with priests and rabbis.'

Growing increasingly alarmed the British pressured the Wafd to stop the strikes that had meanwhile been organized. Leaders of the Wafd were summoned to a meeting with the British authority. At that moment came the first hint that women might soon take over crucial roles from men. When leaders of the Wafd assembled at the Shaarawi house before proceeding together to a meeting with the British, Huda relates, 'My husband gave me an envelope saying, "If we are arrested please give this money to the wife of Saad Pasha. She may need it in our absence." From the window I watched him and the others leave, some with grim smiles and others with heads bent.'

At the meeting the British forced the Wafd to issue an appeal to end the strikes. Huda says,

> The Wafd composed an appeal trying not to compromise their nationalism. When they reached the street an anxious crowd welcomed them. When the appeal for a resumption of order was published the following day, it had no effect because everyone knew that the Wafd had been forced to issue it. The strike not only continued but spread, until virtually all civil servants and workers were involved. The British authority pressured the government to threaten to fire the civil servants if they persisted, and urged them to return to their jobs. They refused, however, and called for the downfall of the government. Rushdi Pasha, the prime minister, then summoned senior government officials in a futile attempt to persuade them to support the government's directive.

Huda and other women, for the first but not last time, also asked for the resignation of the government. The prime minister at the time, Husain Rushdi, was the husband of Huda's late friend and mentor, Eugénie Le Brun. Huda records in her memoirs that when the prime minister received the women's letter he sighed, 'The women want my resignation as well.' He resigned that day. Huda notes, 'The prime minister resigned after receiving an ultimatum from the British and so it served as another form of protest.'

Huda and other women helped keep the strikes alive. Segregation of sex and class broke down as harem women stationed themselves at the doors to government offices urging men not to return to work. 'Women took off their jewellery and offered it to government workers with the plea, "If you want money take this but do not hinder our cause by going back to work under British threat."' She goes on to say, 'Unfortunately, many went back to work and signed papers apologizing for their absence. As I watched the strikers return I was sad yet I could excuse it to some extent since the men had been without salaries, for most their sole income, for a long time.' She adds, 'However, even personal hardship did not prevent more acts of revolt and strikes on the part of all classes.'

The women stepped up their political activities. At the end of 1919 when the Milner Mission arrived in Egypt to investigate the revolution the women mounted another demonstration. Huda recalls, 'We women demonstrated against the Milner Mission. As we drove past the headquarters of the Protectorate we were accosted by British soldiers who jumped on the steps of our carriages taunting and hitting us. In the mêlée a woman's veil was torn from her.' Soon afterwards, the women convened in the Cathedral of Saint Mark. They drafted a resolution 'in the name of the women of Egypt' to send to the British authority protesting that the Milner Mission was out to preserve the British occupation of Egypt. They sent another communication protesting their own maltreatment during the demonstration.[9]

Within a month the women met at the Cathedral once again. Over a thousand women of all classes were reported to have attended. Here Egyptian women for the first time formed a political body. They called it the Wafdist Women's Central Committee to support the Wafd, at the time not yet a year old. Huda was elected president.[10]

Huda at age forty-four. This is one of the first photographs of an unveiled Egyptian woman to appear in local newspapers.

The end of 1920 was a period of strained unity between women and men Wafdists, a strain precipitated by the men's neglect. In October, Wafdist male leaders who had finally managed to get to London for talks, returned with proposed terms for independence to present to the people. The proposal was shown to numerous male groups and organizations but not to the Wafdist Women's Central Committee, who in the words of Huda, 'had worked hard alongside the Wafd in the nationalist movement.' The women took matters into their own hands and got a copy of the proposal themselves. They found the terms inadequate, and published their views in the press.[11] The members of the Wafdist Women's Central Committee also sent a sharp letter to the head of the Wafd. Huda says, 'We criticized the delegates from the Wafd for disregarding our rights and our very existence by neglecting to solicit our views.' Huda signed the letter the Wafdist Women's Central Committee sent to Saad Zaghlul on 12 December. It read:

> We are surprised and shocked by the way we have been treated recently, in contrast to previous treatment and certainly contrary to what we expect from you. You supported us when we created our Committee. Your congratulatory telegrams expressed the finest hopes and most noble sentiments. What makes us all the more indignant is that by disregarding us the Wafd has caused foreigners to disparage the renaissance of women. They claim that our participation in the nationalist movement was merely a ploy to dupe civilized nations into believing in the advancement of Egypt and its ability to govern itself. Our women's renaissance is above that as you well know. At this moment when the future of Egypt is about to be decided, it is unjust that the Wafd, which stands for the rights of Egypt and struggles for its liberation, should deny half the nation its role in that liberation.

The women got a letter of apology from Zaghlul.

There was not only strained unity between women and men Wafdists but strains within male Wafdist ranks. While Wafdist leaders were conferring abroad relations between Huda's husband and Saad Zaghlul deteriorated. Huda displayed considerable political skill in managing to act independently as a Wafdist yet showing loyalty towards her husband. This is illustrated on the occasion of Zaghlul's return to Egypt in April 1921, when Huda as president of the Wafdist Women's Central Committee went to

Safiyya Zaghlul appears unveiled in London in 1921 with Saad Zaghlul and other members of the Wafd during negotiations for independence. In Egypt, Safiyya still veiled while the men discarded their tophats for tarbushes. (See other photograph of Saad Zaghlul p.114)

welcome the president of the Wafd while Ali Shaarawi remained at home.

Huda recounts the incident:

> I was among the delegation of women who went to greet Saad and his wife at their house. We found great crowds of women and men congregating in the two tents, one for women and one for men erected next to the house (segregation was still in force). I felt uncomfortable about being there while my husband, who was instrumental in helping the Wafd gain the trust of the nation, remained at home, neglected by the people. As those thoughts ran through my head, I heard the voice of Sayyid Agha calling to me, 'Saad Pasha is inquiring, "Where is the *raisa* (president), where is the *raisa*?"' However, I preferred to remain on the sidelines, owing

to my awkward position. Saad Pasha made his way out through the lines of women (men in elevated positions were permitted by etiquette formally to visit women or to receive formal visits from women), looking from side to side asking, 'Where is the *raisa*? I wish to offer my thanks.' I congratulated him on his safe return. Afterwards, I asked Sharifa Hanim Riyad and the other women of the Committee to stand in for me and to excuse my departure. They understood my position. The same day, Saad Pasha came to our house and thanked me again for welcoming him, but he did not ask for my husband, which upset me. However, I was glad the following day when he returned and shook hands with Shaarawi Pasha.

Another incident also reveals Huda's political adroitness. When she and other Wafdist women learned that Saad Zaghlul had planned angry demonstrations against the Egyptian prime minister, Adli Yakan, returning to Egypt from abortive negotiations in London, they went to Zaghlul's house to dissuade him. Huda absented herself while the other women talked with Zaghlul because of renewed discord between her husband and the president of the Wafd. She remained in another room with Safiyya Zaghlul, Saad's wife. Huda says, 'When Saad Pasha noticed I was not with the women he insisted on coming to greet me.' While the harem system prevailed, if women and men communicated under ordinary circumstances they did so through a barrier. Huda confides, 'I allowed him to greet me from behind a screen.' Keeping her distance, Huda used the harem screen politically. She continues:

He thanked me for the services I had rendered in strengthening the Wafd and said he wished to reward me. Each of us, I responded, acts out of a sense of duty toward the nation in the hour of need. I have done nothing to deserve thanks or reward. He answered, 'How can that be? You have served the movement. How can I reward you for it?' I seized the moment and said, 'Since you insist upon rewarding me I shall make a request.' He replied, 'With pleasure, what is your wish?' I said, 'Receive Adli Pasha with honour and respect, the way he received you when you returned to Egypt. Stop the plans for the insulting demonstrations being prepared for his welcome.' He remained silent for a moment, and then answered, 'By God, if it were up to me, alone, I would do it to please you, but even if I were to agree to your request the others would not.' I asked who refused him when he wanted something. At that point, Safiyya Hanim[12] rushed toward him saying, 'If you place your hand in Adli's I swear by God, I shall cease to be your wife after what Adli has done.' Saad said to me, 'Did you hear Madame?' 'Yes,' I responded.

When Adli returned to Egypt he was, indeed, badly received and subsequently resigned.

At the end of the year (1921) Huda and other Wafdist women moved to centre stage when Zaghlul was deported after increased political agitation. The Wafdist Women's Central Committee, putting aside their disagreement with Zaghlul, closed ranks and protested in a letter to the British High Commissioner on 25 December signed by Huda Shaarawi. 'You cannot silence the voice of the nation by stifling the voice of the person who speaks for the nation. There are millions who will speak out for liberty and denounce injustice. We shall not cease our vehement protest against the arbitrary and tyrannical measures you take against us – deeds that excite the wrath of the people.'[13]

The women now resorted to new militant tactics. In January 1922 Huda opened her house to a mass meeting of women. They passed resolutions calling for an end to martial law, the abolition of the Protectorate, and opposing the formation of a cabinet while the president of the Wafd was in exile. They forwarded these to the British government. The women also voted for an economic boycott against the British. This involved refusing to buy British goods and withdrawing money from British banks. At the same time the women would campaign to buy Egyptian goods and support Bank Misr, the new Egyptian bank.[14] Although the women used their own private space, the harem, to decide their political moves as meetings were banned, British intelligence penetrated this private world. Copies of discussions of the boycott at a second meeting at Huda's house in the Public Records Office in London attest to this.[15]

The women used their own networks to execute their economic boycott. Women under Islamic law inherit money and property in their own name and in principle may dispose of it as they wish: women, responsible for running households and looking after families, played major roles in consumption. Through their links with middle-class women active in new associations in Cairo and provincial towns, Huda and her friends were able to reach a broad section of the population.[16] The Wafd sent a letter to the women saying, 'We shall never forget your great service when you quickly rose to action with the boycott. It was one of the most powerful weapons in our struggle.' Later, when he was back in Egypt, Zaghlul himself commended the women's boycott.[17]

During the detention and exile of the Wafd leaders, Huda and other women assumed important roles in communications. They kept news flowing between the exiled nationalists and the Egyptian people: they were often a link between the men and the British: they played delicate diplomatic roles connected with the release of the Wafdists, dealt with finances, and monitored the health of the detainees. At the same time, the women kept up the morale of the movement and maintained a stream of political protest. It is not easy to exaggerate the bravery of the women at a time when massive numbers of British troops were in the country, martial law was in effect, meetings were banned, and the press and letters censored.[18]

In the midst of all this the British issued a unilateral declaration of Egyptian independence considerably modified by four Reserved Points. This meant, among other things, the continued stationing of British troops in the country, and left the question of the future fate of the relationship between Egypt and the Sudan in the hands of the British. The women and men of the Wafd opposed these conditions.

In February 1922, Ali Shaarawi died. A widow in mourning, Huda remained at the head of the Wafdist women. She told them at a meeting not long afterwards,

> Neither illness, grief, nor fear of censure can prevent me from shouldering my duty with you in the continuing fight for our national rights. I have vowed to you and to myself to struggle until the end of my life to rescue our beloved country from occupation and oppression. I shall always honour the trust you have placed in me. Let it never be said that there was a woman in Egypt who failed, for personal reasons, to perform her duty to the nation. I would rather die than bring shame upon myself and my sisters. I will remain by your side and at your head through good and bad times, with hope in the future while we defend the rights of

our beloved country. Neither repeated hardships, nor the heavy-handedness of our present government will lessen my will nor deter me from fighting for the full independence of my country.

On this occasion she scorned 'the merely verbal independence of Egypt. Tharwat Pasha (who formed a government on 1 March) now boasts about the independence the imperialists hail as a magnanimous gift. It is no more than a right only partially restored to its owners. We women consider it merely a move to paralyse our national movement and mute our passions.' She continued:

The burden of proof is not upon us. The leader of our national renaissance, Saad Zaghlul Pasha, and other members of the Wafd, are suffering the pain of exile in the Seychelles. Their only guilt was to have demanded independence. Here in Egypt military courts pass judgement on the lives of our sons. Censorship of the press gags our mouths. The prisons are filled with our best men. Special laws are enacted to prevent us from congregating. All this persists despite the conditions Tharwat Pasha laid down for forming a new government, which included the abolition of martial law and of the restrictions upon the freedom of the press and freedom of speech, the return of those in exile, and freeing those detained at home. Such is the subterfuge of our enemy, to trap us in the net of eternal enslavement. I am not implying our ministers were deliberate partners to this, because I refuse, like every other Egyptian, to say there is a single disloyal Egyptian, but I must affirm that the majority of our national demands would have been met if Tharwat Pasha had not agreed to form a government. I think he acted out of naïve trust in the British and faintheartedness.

Ladies, the leaders of our enemy have sensed this weakness in some of our political leaders. They have used these persons as a shield, from behind which they shoot arrows of deceit and cunning. However, the British have failed to reckon with our weapon, the weapon that cannot fail to miss the target, one we have already employed, the lethal weapon of the boycott. Let us aim it again at the face of our enemy and swear not to let it drop until Saad returns and we achieve all our demands. Long live the boycott! Long live unity! Long live Saad and his companions! Long live total independence! Long live the will of Egyptian women![19]

For a good year Huda and the other Wafdist women kept up their political activities on all fronts.

Nabawiyya Musa, Huda, and Saiza Nabarawi attending an International Feminist Meeting in Rome in 1923.

Carrie Chapman Catt, President of the International Alliance of Women wishes Egyptian sisters success.

1923 was a crucial year for Huda and other women. On the fourth anniversary of the day they had emerged from their harems and marched veiled in the streets, Huda led some of these same women in founding the Egyptian Feminist Union. She was elected president. Less than a fortnight later Egyptian women hailed a victory when Saad Zaghlul was released. In April the new constitution declared: 'All Egyptians are equal before the law. They enjoy equally civil and political rights and are equally charged with public duties and responsibilities without distinction of race, language, or religion.' The constitution was not the work of the Wafdists, who scorned the new government charged with writing it, but it seemed to augur well for women. Hope died, however, after just three weeks when the new electoral law granted suffrage to men only. Since the law was the work of the government both Wafdist women and men scorned, the Wafd could not be implicated. Soon after the women had left their seclusion for the arena of public political protest, male leaders of the Wafd had agreed to work for the liberation of women after independence, according to a conversation recorded in Saad Zaghlul's diary.[20] They had yet to show their hand.

In May, Huda led a delegation of three from the Egyptian Feminist Union to a meeting of the International Alliance of Women in Rome. Just going to the meeting was itself a victory for Huda, as well as for Saiza Nabarawi, a young woman in her twenties, the daughter of a late friend of Huda (Adila Nabarawi recalled earlier in the memoirs), and Nabawiyya Musa, a teacher from Alexandria. Three years earlier Huda had formed a delegation from the Wafdist Women's Central Committee to attend the Alliance meeting in Geneva but the women were prevented by their husbands from going. While some might argue that times were better in 1923, it is worth noting that the new delegation was composed of a widow and two single women. It was upon their return from this feminist conference that Huda and Saiza took off their veils in the dramatic incident recounted in the beginning of the Introduction.

Huda refused to sacrifice women's liberation for male political purposes. An episode in the summer of 1923 is telling: she was sailing to Egypt on the same boat that carried Saad Zaghlul, accompanied by his wife, home from exile. Huda's veil now simply covered her head; her face was free. Observing this, Saad asked Huda to help his wife arrange her veil the same way. At Alexandria, Safiyya Zaghlul stood ready to disembark with her face uncovered. When men of the Wafd came aboard to welcome the returning hero and saw Safiyya they said the people would never accept it. She left the boat veiled. Huda, the president of the Wafdist Women's Central Committee, left unveiled.[21]

The Wafd came to power in January 1924. They had gained an overwhelming majority in the Chamber of Deputies and soon after Zaghlul formed a government. The inauguration of Parliament was a landmark and a celebration of national achievement. However, women were barred from the occasion, except as wives of ministers and other high officials. At that moment they had either to go forward or backwards. The day Parliament opened the women were at the gates with pickets. The Wafdist Women's Central Committee and the Egyptian Feminist Union had written nationalist and feminist demands on placards which young girls from the workshops of the Society of the New Women paraded back and forth. The two women's organizations printed a list of thirty-two nationalist and feminist demands and distributed them to Members of Parliament and government officials.

Nevertheless, it was Huda's radical nationalism, not her feminism, which led to her separation from the Wafd. In 1924 the central issue in the relations between Egypt and Britain was the Sudan which had been one of the four Reserved Points in the declaration of independence. Since the late nineteenth century the Sudan had been under the joint rule of the Anglo-Egyptian Condominium but now Britain wished to remove Egypt. The Wafdist government was conciliatory but the Wafdist women adamantly opposed it and called for another anti-British boycott. Six days later on the anniversary of the founding of the Wafd, Huda, the president of the Wafdist Women's Central Committee, was not invited to attend. She protested to Zaghlul, who replied with a face-saving excuse and an apology. Huda had been given a signal and a second chance to march in line with the male Wafd leadership.

Within a week the British sirdar of the Egyptian army and governor-general of the Sudan was killed in Cairo. The British issued a stinging seven-point ultimatum to Egypt. The Women's Boycott Committee telegrammed Zaghlul to refuse the ultimatum. The Egyptian government, however, accepted the first four points requiring an apology, suppression of political demonstrations, a fine and criminal investigation. Huda communicated her disapproval to Zaghlul. In an open letter to the newspaper, *Al-Akhbar*, she said: 'Since you have failed while in public office to fulfil your mandate by positive action, I ask you not to be an obstacle in your country's struggle for liberation . . . I ask you to step down.'[22]

Afterwards Huda resigned as president of the Wafdist Women's Central Committee. From that moment she continued her nationalist activity within the framework of the Egyptian Feminist Union. A final passage in her memoirs captures her sentiments.

> Exceptional women appear at certain moments in history and are moved by special forces. Men view these women as supernatural beings and their deeds as miracles. Indeed, women are bright stars whose light penetrates dark clouds. They rise in times of trouble when the wills of men are tried. In moments of danger, when women emerge by their side, men utter no protest. Yet women's great acts and endless sacrifices do not change men's views of women. Through their arrogance, men refuse to see the capabilities of women. Faced with contradiction, they prefer to raise women above the ordinary human plane instead of placing them on a level equal to their own. Men have singled out women of outstanding merit and put them on a pedestal to avoid recognizing the capabilities of all women. Women have felt this in their souls. Their dignity and self-esteem have been deeply touched. Women reflected on how they might elevate their status and worth in the eyes of men. They decided that the path lay in participating with men in public affairs. When they saw the way blocked, women rose up to demand their liberation, claiming their social, economic, and political rights. Their leap forward was greeted with ridicule and blame, but that did not weaken their will. Their resolve led to a struggle that would have ended in war, if men had not come to acknowledge the rights of women.

From 1923 until her death at sixty-eight in 1947, Huda Shaarawi led a feminist movement in Egypt. All but one of the other ten initial members of the Egyptian Feminist Union were women from the world of the upper-class harem.

The transition of Huda and other feminist pioneers was fraught

Delegates Saiza and Huda, at Rome, 1923.

with contradictions. While active in feminist and nationalist politics and participating in international feminist meetings abroad,
the women in their everyday life continued to face restrictions.
Removing the veil signalled the end of the harem system but the
actual process was piecemeal, slow and painstaking. Old conventions had to be overcome by individual acts rather than formal
demands. Saiza Nabarawi, the editor of *L'Egyptienne* (*The
Egyptian Woman*), the journal of the Feminist Union, told me
some stories about breaking with precedent such as the time Huda
and she attended their first party where men were present (the
other women were all foreigners). It occurred at the Legation of
the United States. Egyptian men showed surprise but nothing
more serious resulted.

The same year (1925), Huda helped start the Club of the

Girls from 'The New Women Society' demanding women's rights at the opening of the New Egyptian Parliament in 1924.

Women's Union, a cultural centre for upper-class women and a successor to the Intellectual Association of Egyptian Women which she had also helped create a decade earlier. Later Huda, remarking to women about the distance they had come, told them how she and the other women had flaunted convention when they acquired premises for the first association. It had been unheard of in 1914 for women to have a meeting place outside the privacy of the harem. She went on to say that they did not dare call the first association a *club* 'because our traditions would not have allowed it'.[23] The women had to know when to act but not to be too explicit about it. In the early 1930s, the Feminist Union moved into its imposing new headquarters in the centre of Cairo. It soon became known as 'The House of the Woman'. The Feminist

Union wanted to carve this on the façade of the building but public objection was so strong that the matter was dropped.[24] Stories like these reveal how difficult it was for women to put the harem years behind them.

But Huda would not be daunted. She was a powerful and charismatic leader. Before the end of the 1920s the Egyptian Feminist Union had, under her direction, grown to some two hundred and fifty members and had attracted middle-class as well as upper-class women. However, staunch activists with sustained commitment like Huda remained relatively few. Huda gave generously of her large fortune to finance the movement. The Feminist Union itself also raised money. The women's funds supported two monthly journals (in French and Arabic), a clinic and dispensary for poor women and children, craft workshops for poor girls, and childcare facilities for working mothers. Financial independence was essential to the longevity and success of the movement.

For Huda, who herself had been married at thirteen, a priority was to have a minimum marriage age set by law. This was achieved during the first year of the movement. The Feminist

Women meeting in Huda's house to plan for the boycott of British goods in 1924.

Union also fought for other changes in family law: within the framework of Islamic law they argued for such things as controls on men's easy access to divorce and a restriction of polygamy. There was no success on either front but their educational demands fared better. In 1924, the first secondary school for girls opened in Shubra (it produced some second-generation feminists) and before the decade had ended the first women had entered the Egyptian university. They were required to sit in the front row in class – a vestige of segregation.

In the 1930s, the feminists focused on work for women in the new textile factories and retail shops and in the expanding educational, health and legal professions. When young women working in Cairo pastry shops took complaints of exploitation directly to Huda herself, she pressured the Labour Office to hire a woman inspector to investigate women's working conditions. In the second half of the 1930s the feminists stepped up the campaign for women's suffrage. In France for a feminist meeting one summer, Huda and other Egyptian feminists even campaigned on behalf of French women who also lacked political rights. Huda also endeavoured to broaden the base of the feminist movement in the second half of the 1930s by reaching out to women in the rural areas. She tried to promote a branch of the Feminist Union in Minya but met with limited response from both local women and Cairo feminists. More successful was the new youth group of the Feminist Union which Hawa Idris headed.

Huda was known not only in Egypt and in the international feminist community – through ties with the International Alliance of Women of which she became a vice-president – but also in other Arab countries. In the late 1930s, when political crises mounted in Palestine, Arab women contacted Huda for help. She took political action and collected funds to send to Palestine. At the same time she organized a conference of Arab women in Cairo to deal with the Palestinian situation. The women's collective nationalist activity led to collective Arab feminism in a manner reminiscent of Egyptian women's earlier move from nationalist to feminist activism. Huda organized a second conference of Arab women in Cairo in 1944, where the women formed the Arab Feminist Union and elected Huda president.

Through her feminism Huda had taken charge of her life and had broken through barriers dividing gender and class upheld by

Huda at the door to her Cairo house wearing the Nishan al-Kamal, *the highest state decoration of Egypt for services rendered to the country (taken in 1945, two years before her death).*

the old harem system. Within the upper class, barriers between women and men had diminished and in the context of feminist struggle class boundaries between women lessened. Towards the end of her life, the state awarded Huda Shaarawi its highest decoration. Yet it withheld from her political rights. It was a symbol of the contradictions with which she and other women had to live.

NOTES

INTRODUCTION

1. See Lucie Duff Gordon, *Letters from Egypt*, London, 1865, reprinted, 1983.
2. See Afaf Lutfi al-Sayyid Marsot, *Egypt in the Reign of Muhammad Ali*, Cambridge, 1984; E. R. J. Owen, *Cotton and the Egyptian Economy, 1820–1914*, London, 1969; Janet Abu Lughod, *Cairo: 1001 Years of the City Victorious*, Princeton, 1971; and Stanley Lane Poole, *Cairo Fifty Years Ago*, London, 1896.
3. On the Circassian heritage, see contemporary accounts in Harvey, *Turkish Harems and Circassian Homes*, London, 1871 and E. Spencer, *Travels in Circassia*, 2 vols., London, 1839.
4. Ali Pasha Mubarak, *Tariq al-Hijja wa al-Tamrin ala Qawaid al-Lugha al-Arabiyya (The Way to Spell and Practice according to the Rules of the Arabic Language)*, Cairo, 1869; and Rifai al-Tahtawi, *Al-Murshid al-Amin lil-Banat wa al-Banin (The Faithful Guide for Girls and Boys)*, Cairo, 1875.
5. On Muhammad Abduh and Qasim Amin see Albert Hourani, *Arabic Thought in the Liberal Age*, Cambridge, 1983.
6. For a detailed study of this subject based on primary sources see Alexander Schölch, *Egypt for the Egyptians! The Socio-Political Crisis in Egypt 1878–1882*, London, 1981.
7. On the life and writing of Malak Hifni Nasif, see Majd al-Din Hifni Nasif, *Athar Bahithat al-Badiyya Malak Hifni Nasif, 1886–1918 (The Legacy of Bahithat al-Badiyya Malak Hifni Nasif)*, Cairo, 1962.
8. On the Wafd see Lou Cantori, 'The Organizational Basis of an Elite Political Party: The Egyptian Wafd', Ph.D. dissertation, University of Chicago, 1966.

PART ONE

1. Following the death of Idris, his daughters, Hawa and Huriyya, went to Egypt where they were raised by their elder cousin, Huda Shaarawi. Hawa, following her cousin, became active in the Egyp-

tian feminist movement; she was the president of the *Shaqiqat*, the youth group of the Egyptian Feminist Union.

2. Shaikh Shamil al-Daghistani was one of three principal leaders in the Caucasus who fought against the Russians.

3. Ilhami Pasha was the son of the Viceroy of Egypt, Abbas I. His daughter, Amina, became the wife of Khedive Taufiq.

4. Hawa and Huriyya Idris, daughters of Iqbal's younger brother Idris, were later brought to Egypt and reared by Huda Shaarawi in her household following their father's death.

5. On Sultan Pasha see Qallini Fahmi, *Souvenirs du Khedive Ismail au Khedive Abbas II*, pp. 23–25, 82–91, and *Mudhakkirat (Memoirs)*, Cairo, 1943; F. Robert Hunter, *Egypt under the Khedives 1805–1879: From Household Government to Modern Bureaucracy*, Pittsburg, 1984 (excellent on all the leading officials of the period), and 'The Making of a Notable Politician: Muhammad Sultan Pasha (1825–1884)', *International Journal of Middle East Studies*, vol. 15, 1983, pp. 537–44; Abd al-Aziz Rifai, *Sultan Pasha Amam al-Tarikh (Sultan Pasha in History)*, Cairo, n.d.; Alexander Scholch, op. cit.

6. Qallini Pasha Fahmi, who lived to be 100 years old, was secretary to Sultan Pasha in the latter's later years.

7. Hasan al-Sharii Pasha, who was from a large landowning family of Upper Egypt, was a member of the Council of Deputies in 1881 and Minister of *Awqaf* (pious endowments) in 1882.

8. This house which still stands today is pleasantly situated on the east bank of the Nile. Of modest proportions the exterior resembles an ancient Egyptian temple while the interior is laid out in the manner of a traditional country house.

9. Muhammad Ibn Ahmad al-Hatib al-Ibshihi (1388–1446) compiled this collection of *belles-lettres*, essays on ethics and anecdotes. It was republished in 1851 in Bulaq and was later translated into French by G. Rat and published in 1899 in Paris and Toulon.

10. Nubar Pasha, born in Turkey of a respected Armenian family, had a distinguished career in Egypt; he was president of the Council of Ministers under Khedive Ismail. Sharif and Riyad Pasha, both prominent statesmen, were presidents of the Council of Ministers, the former under Khedive Ismail and Taufiq, and the latter under Taufiq.

11. Ismail Pasha Saddiq was Director of Finances and Inspector General of Egypt under Khedive Ismail.

PART TWO

1. *Umm Kabira* (Big Mother) was the affectionate name for Hasiba, who was a wife of Sultan Pasha, older than Huda's mother, Iqbal.

2. On the precedence of male children in the harem, see Ellen Chennells, *Recollections of an Egyptian Princess by her English Governess*, 2 vols., London, 1893, p. 64, who observed in Khedive Ismail's harem, ' . . . as children in their mother's harem Ibrahim Pasha, though a year younger than his sister, was put first in everything.'

3. At the beginning of the nineteenth century, the European doctors Muhammad Ali had brought to Egypt to take care of his troops began to treat the women of his family and some women of upper-class families as well.

4. Bashir Agha was an Ethiopian slave freed upon the death of Sultan Pasha. Two years before Huda Shaarawi was born the castration of men was outlawed but the practice took time to die out. Richard Burton, who studied the matter, writing in 1885 said that men were still being castrated in Nubia and other parts of the Sudan, and in Ethiopia. See Richard Burton, *Love, War and Fancy: The Social and Sexual Customs of the East*, ed. Kenneth Walker, London, 1964, pp. 220–5.

5. For accounts of education in the harem see Ellen Chennells (she was governess to Princess Zainab, the youngest daughter of Khedive Ismail), op. cit. See also Emine Foat Tugay, *Three Centuries: Family Chronicles of Turkey and Egypt*, London, 1963; and Sophie Babazogli, *L'Education de la jeune fille musulman en Egypt*, Cairo, 1928, a sketchy account.

6. The memorization of the entire Koran by girls in the harem appears to have been uncommon; however, it was usual for them to memorize various *ayas* or verses.

7. Ibn Muhammad Abd al-Rabbih is the author of *Al-Iqd al-Farid (The Unique Necklace)*, an encyclopaedia of knowledge for the well-informed man.

8. Her name would suggest that she or her forebears came from North Africa. Women poets were of a different class from story-tellers and, if accomplished, might attract an audience of men.

9. The Jabalaiyya was a hill on the then grassy island in the Nile called al-Jazira (later part of the fashionable enclave, Zamalek). It had not been customary for females and males, even children, to be seen outside the harem. Ellen Chennells, op. cit., vol. 1, p. 5, relates that when Ismail's children, Zainab and Ibrahim, went out for their lessons, although from the same palace, 'they were always in separate carriages . . . It was Eastern etiquette that, however nearly connected, they should be strangers to each other out of doors.'

10. *Id al-Saghir*, the Minor Feast, occurs on the first three days of the Muslim month of *Shawwal*, celebrating the end of Ramadan. Women of all classes visited relatives and close friends, and the

tombs of deceased relatives during the feast days. *Yaum Ashura*, the Tenth of *Muharram*, the first Muslim month, commemorates the slaying at Kerbala of Husain, the grandson of the Prophet Muhammad. The Twenty-seventh of *Rajab*, the seventh month in the Muslim year, is the feast of *Lailat al-Isra wa al-Miraj*, celebrating the miraculous flight of the Prophet Muhammad through the skies to Jerusalem and into the heavens.

11. The *Mulid al-Nabi*, the Birthday of the Prophet, is celebrated the eleventh night of *Rabia al-Awwal*, the third month in the Muslim year. Some eighty *mulids* were celebrated in the Egypt of Huda's day according to J. W. McPherson, *The Moulids of Egypt*, Cairo, 1941. Especially popular in Cairo was the *mulid* of Sayyida Zainab, a granddaughter of the Prophet Muhammad and daughter of Ali.

12. The canal going from the Nile east in the direction of the Citadel was dammed when the river began to rise, and when the water reached a certain height the dam was cut to flood the land for irrigation. Since ancient times, the waters of the Nile, source of life to Egyptians, have been propitiated. The cutting of the canal was celebrated with ritual of pre-Islamic origin. Before Islam a young woman dressed as a bride was sacrificed to the river; afterwards an effigy was substituted.

13. There are photographs of houses and gardens like this in Arnold Wright (ed.), *Twentieth Century Impressions of Egypt*, London, 1909.

14. Slavery was outlawed in Egypt in 1877 by a protocol signed by Khedive Ismail and castration was likewise prohibited. It was virtually impossible, however, to put an immediate end to slavery. The lucrative slave trade was difficult to stamp out and slaves already in households had to be freed by their master or go away of their own accord. Huda Shaarawi's father arranged to have his slaves freed upon his death which occurred in 1884.

15. Ferdinand de Lesseps was the builder of the Suez Canal.

16. Amina Hanim Afandi (1874–1931) was the mother of Khedive Abbas Hilmi II and a great benefactress known as 'The Mother of Benefactors'. She supported the Egyptian Feminist Union.

17. This would have happened customarily at the age of nine or ten when girls put on the veil for the first time, signifying their entry into the world of adult women and into a state of seclusion and segregation from males other than close relatives.

18. It was customary for the prospective groom to make a gift of jewellery, the *nishan*, to the woman he intended to marry near the time of betrothal. Huda's failure to detect the significance of the gift of jewellery made to her at the time indicates the extreme secrecy her mother maintained with regard to her plan for her daughter's

142

marriage. With no older sisters in the same household she had no
occasion to observe such procedures before.

19. Khedive Taufiq frequented Helwan for its thermal baths. Members
of his family, wealthy Egyptians and foreigners flocked to Helwan
especially during the annual forty-day residence of the court there.
The khedive died in Helwan the year Huda was married. See Emine
Foat Tugay, op. cit., p. 194.

20. A *wakil*, a man designated as an agent, represented the woman
signing betrothal and marriage certificates on her behalf.

21. It was customary for the bride to move to the household of
her husband's family where her mother-in-law reigned supreme.
Huda Shaarawi, however, remained in her late father's house. Her
husband's usual residence was in Upper Egypt where he had lived
with his former wife and three children.

22. Huda Shaarawi was thirteen when she was married, a common
marriage age for girls of all classes during the nineteenth century. It
was also common for girls to marry their cousins although it was
thought by some to be less prevalent among Cairenes than other
Egyptians. Weddings of the upper classes were lavish affairs lasting
three days or more.

23. Writing particular stipulations into marriage contracts, such as
demanding monogamy, as in Huda's case, was permitted but it was
not widely done.

PART THREE

1. The Khedivial Opera House was built in 1869 to celebrate the
opening of the Suez Canal. It was equipped with harem boxes fitted
out with grilles reached by a private staircase enabling women
to attend performances. Adila Hanim Nabarawi, the daughter of
Yusif Pasha Nabarawi and his French wife, was raised in Paris. She
had returned to Egypt to marry her cousin, Ibrahim Nabarawi,
when she and Huda became friends. Adila had no children but took
her infant niece, Zainab Murad, to Paris to raise. Renamed Saiza
Nabarawi, she later became a staunch feminist alongside Huda.

2. Under an institution known as *bait al-taa* (literally, house of obedi-
ence) a wife who had left her husband's house without permission
could be required to return by force if necessary.

3. Ramleh, to the east of Alexandria, was a summer retreat for wealthy
Egyptians and foreigners. It now forms part of Alexandria.

4. Muslim women, according to the Shariah, Islamic religious law,
enjoy full use of their money and property. They can buy and sell,

in short, conduct business of their own without the permission or interference of husbands or male relatives. The exercise of that right was another matter and a question that requires study.

5. When a husband and wife are separated, according to the principle of Islamic law, custody of young children goes to the mother while older children go to the father. The ages of custody vary among the different schools of Islamic law. However, boys are entrusted to their father's care at an earlier age than girls. In Egypt, before the feminists led by Huda agitated for change in the 1920s mothers had custody of daughters until nine and sons until seven.

6. Her former husband from a Sharifian family of the *Hidjaz* claiming descent from the Prophet Muhammad carried a revered name associated with *baraka* or blessing. It was Atiyya Hanim's association with this name that gave her special status.

7. Madame Rushdi, born Eugénie Le Brun, was raised in France. Husain Rushdi Pasha became prominent in Egyptian political life. He was prime minister in four governments between 1914 and 1917.

8. In the 1890s Eugénie Le Brun began the first salon for women in Cairo. Earlier Princess Nazli Fazil (whose father was Prince Mustafa Fazil and uncle was the late Khedive Ismail) had begun a salon for statesmen, politicians, writers, journalists, and intellectuals, both Egyptian and European, but no Egyptian women attended it. After Eugénie Le Brun's day, the Lebanese writer and poet, May Ziyada, began her highly acclaimed literary salon which also was principally attended by men.

9. The Imam al-Shafai burial ground at the eastern extremity of Cairo on the Muqqatam Hills is the city's main Muslim cemetery.

10. *Harem et les musulmanes*, Paris, 1902, as indicated, an act of cultural defence, described the social structure and habits of the upper-class women. *Les repudiées*, Paris, 1908, demonstrated that lower-class women suffered from both class and patriarchal oppression in seeking justice at court.

11. Rudah, at the southern tip of a small island in the Nile south of Jazira Island, was built up early in the nineteenth century. Ibrahim Pasha, the son of Muhammad Ali, built a large garden there and wealthy Turks and Egyptians soon followed his example. In the second half of the nineteenth century Rudah declined in importance as the upper classes moved to the new area of Ismailiyya. Bab al-Khalq, developed under the encouragement of Khedive Ismail, was in this area and the site of *Dar al-Kutub*, the national library founded in 1870.

PART FOUR

1. It was customary for upper-class women to give their infants over to a wet nurse.
2. *Dahabiyyas* or houseboats owned by the wealthy were moored in the Nile for recreational use. Many were anchored near Zamalek which from the end of the nineteenth century became an enclave of foreigners, especially the British. *Feluccas* or sailing boats were used by the poorer classes for crossing the Nile and transporting themselves or goods up and down the river.
3. In 1924, a year after Huda founded the Egyptian Feminist Union, it opened a dispensary for poor women and children. Dr Hess was among the volunteer doctors.
4. Buyuk Deree, a village on the Bosporus was a fashionable summer spot for the wealthy. Many European embassies had summer residences there. A *konak* is a wooden house; the one Huda stayed in was in the hills above Buyuk Deree overlooking the Bosporus. The houses referred to as 'kings palaces' along the shore were *yalis*, ornate wooden mansions built at the edge of the water.
5. The *kalfa* was the head of the female servants in the harem. In Ottoman imperial and Egyptian khedivial households she performed various ceremonial functions such as the one described here.
6. Marguerite Clement taught at the Lycée de Jeunes Filles at Bordeaux and was a feminist and pacifist.
7. Princess Ain al-Hayat was married to Husain Kamil who became Sultan of Egypt from 1914 to 1917.
8. *Al-Jarida*, a journal founded in 1907 and edited by Ahmad Lutfi al-Sayyid, was the paper of the *Umma* party. The journal supported the liberation of Egyptian women. It was open to women writers and the offices of the journal were made available to women for talks. The Egyptian university was founded in 1908; it was expanded in 1923 and called Fuad the First University and after the revolution of 1952 became known as Cairo University.
9. Bahithat al-Badiyya, the pen name of Malak Hifni Nasif (1886–1918), a graduate of the Saniyya Teachers' School, a writer and a feminist, was the first Egyptian woman to make public demands for the liberation of women. She did this at the Egyptian Congress in Heliopolis in 1911.
10. The Foundling Home created at the end of the nineteenth century in memory of the late Lady Cromer, wife of the British commissioner of Egypt, Lord Cromer (1883–1907), led to the formation of the Lady Cromer Society by British and European women whose principal activity was running the home and later a dispensary for poor mothers and children.

11. Avril de Sainte Croix was president of *Le Conseil national des femmes françaises* (est. 1901), a non-suffragist organization affiliated to the International Council of Women. She was active in the peace movement and an ardent campaigner against prostitution.

12. Wagida Khulusi became a charter member of the Egyptian Feminist Union in 1923.

EPILOGUE

1. For a historian's account of the women's demonstration see Abd al-Rahman al-Rafii, *Thaurat Sana 1919 (The 1919 Revolution)*, Cairo, 1946, 2 vols, vol. 1, pp. 137–40; for interviews fifty years later with women who participated in the events of 1919 see Naila Alluba, Muhammad Rifaat, *et al.*, 'Thaura 1919 Rafaat al-Hijab wa al-Yashmak an Wajh al-Mara al-Misriyya' (The 1919 Revolution Lifted the Veil and Yashmak from the Face of the Egyptian Woman), *al-Musawwar*, 7 March 1969.

2. Everything by Huda Shaarawi, unless otherwise indicated, comes from her memoirs.

3. Wagida Khulusi became a founding member of the Egyptian Feminist Union.

4. Regina Khayyat was also a founder of the Egyptian Feminist Union.

5. Thomas Russell, *Egyptian Service*, London, 1949, pp. 46–7.

6. The next women's demonstration took place on 20 March 1919, see al-Rafii, op. cit., pp. 194–5.

7. Letter from Thomas Russell to his father, est. date, 1 April 1919, in Russell Papers, Middle East Centre, St Antony's College, Oxford.

8. For an account of the funeral of the 28-year-old widow whose coffin was wrapped in the Egyptian flag, see Ahmad Shafiq, *Hauliyyat Misr al-Siyasiyya (Political Chronicles of Egypt)*, Cairo, 1926, 1st ed., vol. 1, pp. 260–61.

9. Milner Papers at New College, Oxford, Box 164, vol. 12(c), no. 12, communication, 12/12/19 from Women of Egypt, St Mark's Cathedral and no. 56, communication 8/1/20 from Ladies Committee of Egyptian Delegation, St Mark's Cathedral.

10. According to Saad Zaghlul's secretary, the idea to form the Wafdist Women's Central Committee was Zaghlul's but he himself never makes this claim; see Muhammad Ibrahim al-Jaziri, *Saad Zaghlul: Dhikriyyat Tarikhiyya Tarifa (Saad Zaghlul: Interesting Historical Memoirs)*, Cairo, n.d., pp. 207–8.

11. For other reactions see Afaf Lutfi al-Sayyid Marsot, *Egypt's Liberal Experiment 1922–1936*, Berkeley, 1977, p. 53, who says, 'Public

reaction was distinctly cool ...'; and Jacques Berque, *Egypt: Imperialism and Revolution*, trans. J. Stewart, London, 1972, who relates, 'Lawyers first: these supported the Wafd's attitude. The Legislative Council accepted almost unanimously. Religious and spiritual leaders also approved, with only a few reservations. Members of the judiciary, of provincial councils, of municipal authorities all gave their support; only the Watani party dissented, pointing out the all too real risk of a swindle ... ,' p. 320.

12. Safiyya Hanim, the wife of Saad Zaghlul was born in 1876 in Cairo. Her father, Mustafa Pasha Fahmi, was three times prime minister. She was raised in an upper-class harem, given an education at home and in 1896 at the age of twenty, old for the times, married Saad Zaghlul, a talented middle-class lawyer at the National Court of Appeals. Safiyya devoted herself totally to her husband's career. During periods of his exile, when not sharing it with him, she stood in as his surrogate in Egypt. For more about her, see Fina Gued Vidal, *Safia Zaghlul*, Cairo, n.d.

13. Huda Shaarawi to Allenby, High Commissioner, 25 December 1921, Political Views and Activities of Egyptian Women, Consular and Embassy Archives File 14083, Foreign Office 141, Box 511, Public Records Office, London.

14. According to the private papers of Huda Shaarawi, she herself bought 250 shares. Her brother, Umar Sultan, had been among those who had helped capitalize the bank at its foundation. See Eric Davis, *Challenging Colonialism: Bank Misr and Egyptian Industrialization, 1920–1941*, Princeton, 1983.

15. 'Decision of the Women's Central Committee of the Delegation', Cairo, 7 February 1922 (meeting held on 3 February 1922), Political Views and Activities of Egyptian Women, Consular and Embassy Archives, File 14083, Foreign Office 141, Box 511, Public Records Office, London.

16. Among the women's associations were the Society of the New Woman, the Society of the Renaissance of the Egyptian Woman, and the Society of Mothers of the Future in Cairo, and the Women's Union of Minya, the Women's Union in Asyut, and the Society of Union and Progress in Tanta.

17. Letter from Wasif Ghali on behalf of the Egyptian Wafd to Huda Shaarawi in *Majmuaa al-Khutab Alati Ulqiyat fi Ijtima al-Sayyidat al-Misriyyat bi Dar al-Marhum Husain Basha Abu Usba Yaum al-Jumaa 5 Mayu 1922 (Collection of speeches given at the Egyptian women's meeting at the house of the late Husain Pasha Abu Usba on Friday, 5 May 1922)*, pp. 27–8. Muhammad Ibrahim al-Jaziri, op. cit., pp. 103–6.

18. Safiyya Zaghlul issued communiqués to the public to help keep the nationalist cause alive. She also kept attention focused on

her husband as the leader of the nationalist struggle. She had a great appeal among Egyptians who called her *Umm al-Masriyyin* (colloquial transliteration), Mother of Egyptians. Louise Majorelle Ghali, the French wife of Wafdist leader, Wasif Ghali, was among the women active in maintaining communications with the exiled Wafdists who included her husband. Documents in the Ghali family private papers were made available to me by Mirit Ghali.

19. Speech of the president in *Majmuaa al-khutab* ... (see note 17), pp. 6–10.

20. Saad Zaghlul, *Mudhakirrat (Memoirs)*, National Archives, the Citadel, Cairo, notebook 39 (9 June 1920 – 7 June 1921), entry for 24 November 1920, p. 2380. Reference provided by Abd al-Khaliq Lashin.

21. Personal communication by Saiza Nabarawi.

22. *Al-Akhbar*, 24 November 1924.

23. Huda Shaarawi, 'Kalima al-Sayyida al-Jalila Huda Hanim Shaarawi,' (The lecture of her excellency, Huda Shaarawi) *al-Misriyya*, 15 February 1937, p. 13.

24. Personal communication from Saiza Nabarawi, Cairo, 13 March 1972; Myriam Harrey, 'La femme orientale et son destin: l'Egyptienne,' *Journal de la femme*, Paris, 21 July 1934 (interview with Saiza Nabarawi).

APPENDIX

SULTAN PASHA AND THE URABI REVOLUTION (1881–2)

I have read the memoirs of the late Urabi Pasha which the news-papers published in a way to please particular people in power at the time. When they were no longer in power, Urabi's son, Abd al-Sami Afandi, came to me for help in publishing his father's memoirs in a book. When I showed bewilderment at the curious request to finance the publication of memoirs that had slandered my father and discredited his patriotism, he agreed to make dele-tions. This proposal – more extraordinary than the first – amazed me all the more. I was sure if he was so willing to make changes in the memoirs to obtain money to publish them he must, for a similar reason, have inserted the slander about my father. In dis-gust, I refused his request for help.

I regret that this occurred orally because had it been put in writing it would have proved how distorted the so-called memoirs of Urabi Pasha were. I also regret that some of the distinguished men of Egypt who had been devoted followers of Urabi allowed partisan feelings to colour their judgement. They did not appre-ciate my father's nationalism. People deluded by appearances as far as Urabi was concerned supported the compilation of his memoirs.

I now turn to the testimony of Qallini Fahmi Pasha, a man of integrity, who worked with my father, knew him well, and was around during these events:

I have read an article signed by Abd al-Sami Urabi in the newspaper *Al-Mahrusa*, on 21 November 1923. I address only that which concerns the late Sultan Pasha.

The author of the article claims he does not wish to open a distressing topic – that is the question of the late Sultan Pasha – but since Abd al-Sami Urabi has raised it I am obliged to state that in this article Urabi writes that Sultan Pasha, a leader in the nationalist movement, had

thought that through the talents of Urabi Pasha and the strength of the
army he could become president of a new Parliament and that the
leadership of the nationalist party would go to him owing to his rank and
wealth. Thus, he offered Urabi every support, but when he heard people
frequently praise Urabi he grew jealous. Moreover, his wish to become a
member of Mahmud Sami Pasha's cabinet was not fulfilled. Therefore,
he set out to alienate members of the Council of Deputies and others
from Urabi, but failed because all classes in the country clung to Urabi.

Let me note that the Urabi movement arose in opposition to the
tyranny of Turkish and Circassian army officers, who constituted a
quasi-occupation of the country and monopolized both military and civil
posts. Egyptians for example, could not rise higher than the rank of
colonel. The Urabi movement aimed to rid government departments of
Turkish and Circassian officials as well as many high-ranking Egyptian
notables.

Sultan Pasha assisted the Urabi movement through his considerable
power and influence. I was one of his supporters while he was active in
the Urabi movement, just as I had been a dear friend of Urabi Pasha and
many of the distinguished officers who participated in the movement. In
this connection, I wish to discuss historical events of which I, myself,
was a part. I do so only to preserve the truth for posterity.

I answer Abd al-Sami al-Urabi by demonstrating that his statements
concerning the late Sultan Pasha do not correspond to the facts. At the
beginning of the nationalist movement I do not deny that Urabi Pasha
rendered admirable services to the nation. But his intoxication with early
success eventually led to anarchy and failure, as I shall explain.

Sultan Pasha occupied the post of inspector-general of Upper Egypt.
The *umdas* (mayors) and notables of the administrative districts of Upper
Egypt, as was the population at large, were subject to him. He had great
authority and wielded immense power, and therefore had no need of the
influence of others to attain high position. When the Urabi movement
began he saw it as an opportunity to help his country. He devoted
himself totally to the movement, not in order to gain a position – he
already held one of the most important positions in the country – but
because of what the movement stood for: helping free Egypt from the
domination of the Turks. I affirm this for the memory of the late Sultan
Pasha. Anyone who has known Sultan Pasha, as I have, knows he was a
devoted patriot who rendered his country the most noble services. There
may have been no Egyptian who has served his country as Sultan Pasha
has.

When the Parliament was formed Sultan Pasha was elected president.
It makes no sense to maintain that someone who is president of Parliament would seek to become a minister in Mahmud Sami Pasha's cabinet,

as the author of the article maintains, since the former position is higher than the latter. Abd al-Sami's assertion that Sultan Pasha possessed great prestige and authority itself negates the argument that he sought prestige and authority through the Urabists.

The Urabists succeeded in bringing about the downfall of the Turks and Circassians and, through the power of the army, were able to form a Parliament which enacted a number of beneficial laws. They then began to oppose the khedive, himself, aiming to seize the throne.

I recall having been with Sultan Pasha at home in his *sarai* when Urabi Pasha and a number of army officers appeared demanding that Parliament be convened immediately. Sultan Pasha objected, 'The regular parliamentary period is over. If an important issue arises outside this period, the law requires a khedival decree in order to call an extraordinary session.' He asked, 'What makes it necessary to reconvene Parliament?' They answered him brusquely, 'A khedival decree is not required for a parliamentary session — it must be convened because we demand it.' Sultan Pasha inquired again what was so urgent and was told, 'The khedive's removal.' He asked, 'Was the khedive appointed by the Egyptian Parliament and is it empowered to depose him?' They retorted, 'We do not wish to debate. We wish to act.' Sultan Pasha continued, 'Have you decided upon a successor to the khedive if Parliament were to depose him?' Urabi waited for them to say he would succeed but no one uttered a word. They then conferred with each other and announced, 'We shall postpone things until tomorrow. Tonight we shall choose a successor.'

They left the *sarai* of Sultan Pasha and proceeded to the house of Urabi Pasha where top officers met to discuss the matter. In a heated exchange that night, Mahmud Pasha Sami al-Barudi proclaimed, 'I am most deserving to be the successor, as I am of royal descent.' Urabi said, 'I am the head of the nationalist movement and the one who created it,' while others made various claims. Finally, Tulba Ismat said, 'We have important aims to achieve and should cooperate as equals instead of putting ourselves one above the other. It would be better to transform the provinces into khedivates and each become a khedive!'

Urabi Pasha lost hope of being successor. Some thought that the status quo should be maintained — that the khedive should be left on the throne until a better opportunity arose. Urabi Pasha then returned to the *sarai* of Sultan Pasha and thanked him for the circumspect manner in which he dealt with their demand, for had he complied with their request a bloody struggle would have broken out among them for the position of leadership.

Sultan Pasha pondered these matters and felt that the Urabists were not helping their country as he had hoped they would; on the contrary, personal gain had flamed in all of them. 'Now that we have acquired a national constitution and set up the basic rules for government,' he said, 'the Egyptian army should go no further because the foreigners have grown very uneasy about the problem of permanent military control.' The Urabists did not like this and took it as a betrayal. Ignoring his advice they continued to threaten the throne, arousing the anxieties of the khedive, who soon sought assistance from Europe to guard the throne from danger and save the country from anarchy.

France and Britain heard the call. Britain acted but France did not intervene. The Urabists immediately placed Egypt under martial law, forcing the countryside to provision the army with grain, livestock, and anything else it needed. The Urabists seized all government posts, and began to dismiss persons in authority. They replaced governors of provinces and other officials with decrees issued in the name of the 'Protector of Egypt', Afandina Urabi Pasha.

Meanwhile they declared a state of war with Britain. When the British fleet arrived and the army intervened against Urabi, the Supreme Council, under the direction of the khedive, met in Alexandria and decided to dispatch the late Sultan Pasha – then with the khedival entourage – to Cairo to take charge of the government in the name of the khedive. He was ordered to go immediately lest the capital be without a representative of the khedive. When Urabi heard this he ordered the governor of Minya, Ismail Bey al-Qiyasi, to expropriate Sultan Pasha's grain, horses, and other livestock and send them to the army stores. He also ordered Sultan Pasha's house in Minya to be sealed shut with red wax until further notice.

When the British entered Egypt Sultan Pasha wanted to know their intentions. General Wolseley, commander of the expeditionary force, and Sir Edward Malet, the representative of the government, said they had a mandate to suppress the Urabi revolt and safeguard the throne. When that was achieved they would depart. They confirmed this to the late Sultan Pasha, who passionately loved his country and feared the spectre of British domination. Sultan Pasha would never have opposed Turkish occupation, which he saw as a calamity for the country, only to support British occupation.

Finally, let me stress that the accusations Abd al-Sami Bey and others hurled against the late Sultan Pasha are totally out of keeping with his character and actions. A loyal patriot, deeply concerned for the welfare of the people, he was scrupulous in his conduct, a man of lofty spirit and high principles who was courageous and heroic. There was scarcely anyone like him in the entire country. In the service of truth and history, and moved by the duty of the friendship that has bound me to Sultan Pasha I have felt obligated to reveal things as they were.

I should like to add a few words of my own. During the Urabi revolt and after the arrival of the British, Urabi Pasha ordered Ismail Bey al-Qiyasi, the governor of Minya, to confiscate my father's properties – crops, horses, and the like – and to dispatch them to the army stores and to close Father's house in Minya with red sealing wax until his actions could be investigated. I heard from relatives and servants that members of the household fled to nearby villages and some took refuge in the *jabal* (the long mountainous ridge on the east bank of the Nile across the river). My mother and some of the others stayed with their tenants until the latter could no longer contain their fears of reprisals from Urabi.

Meanwhile, crowds took possession of my father's *sarai* in Cairo. They squatted and plundered, according to my nurse, who witnessed them taking over our rooms and tethering their animals in the garden until the place began to look like the *Suk al-Asr*.

Qallini Fahmi Pasha told me that when security was re-established after the routing and exile of Urabi, the government ordered the payment of 10,000 pounds to my father as indemnity for the material damages he had sustained. Followers of Urabi, who did not know the facts, seized upon this in order to malign my father, saying the money was a reward for collaborating with Khedive Taufiq to aid the entry of the British into Egypt. Even if it were to be imagined – and it is impossible – that my father would hand over the independence of his country in exchange for money, he would not have sold Egypt for such a ridiculous amount. The insignificance of the sum alone should indeed be proof of their slander. My father was perhaps shortsighted at first when, like others, he believed in Urabi. However, he later dropped his criticism of the khedive because he feared that foreign power, alarmed by the anarchy in Egypt and the martial rule, would interfere in the affairs of the country and cause its ruin. Anyone with common sense will understand that my father acted prudently. As long as Urabi continued his provocations, which he did despite weaknesses and insufficient preparation, it was inevitable that the British would enter Egypt. My father preferred the British to enter as friends, in defence of the throne and guaranteeing security, rather than as conquerors. When the British set foot on Egyptian soil, however, they regarded it as an invasion and treated the country as a minion of their empire.

GLOSSARY

TITLES AND PROFESSIONS: FEMALE

Abla   older sister (Turkish)
Anisa   Miss
Dada   nanny (Turkish)
Dallala   woman pedlar
Hanim   married lady (Turkish)
Haram   wife of
Kalfa   head of female household staff (Turkish)
Raisa   president
Sayyida   Mrs
Sharifa   female descendant of the Prophet, Muhammad
Sitt   married lady
Umm   mother (*umm kabira*: big mother or *Umm* Ismail: Mother of Ismail)
Walda   mother of ruler (Turkish)

TITLES AND PROFESSIONS: MALE

Agha   eunuch, guardian of women in the household (Turkish)
Bey   title conferred by the ruler, usually connected with high political or administrative office (Turkish)
Imam   leader of mosque congregation or leader in prayer
Jaffir   guard of property
Khedive   title of viceroy of Egypt used from 1867–1914 (Turkish)
Pasha   lord or sir, title conferred by the ruler (Turkish)
Qahawagi   man who makes coffee; an important part of ritual for receiving guests was to offer freshly made coffee (Turkish)
Sayyid   Mr
Shaikh   a man who has memorized the Koran or is generally learned in religion, a graduate of al-Azhar (thousand-year-old mosque-university in Cairo), an elder
Umda   mayor or village headman
Wakil   agent or deputy (a male deputy would sign the contract of marriage for a bride)

GENERAL TERMS

Ashura   a wheat pudding with nuts and dried fruits

Aya   verse of Koran

Baraka   blessing or grace

Basturma   dried beef preserved with salt and spices, a Turkish specialty also popular in Egypt

Daqn al-basha   literally, 'the pasha's beard'

Daira   estate

Dahabiyya   houseboat

Dirham   old Arabic silver coin still circulating in late nineteenth century Egypt

Diwan   collection of poems

Faddan   a measure of land equal to 1.038 acres

Fallah   peasant

Fatta   savoury pastry filled with cheese, meat or spinach

Haj   pilgrimage to Mecca

Id   feast

Iftar   meal breaking the fast at sunset during Ramadan

Izar   outer black cloak worn by women of upper classes

Izba   country estate or farm

Jabal   mountain

Jamaiyya   society or association

Kiosk   an open pavilion often placed in mansion gardens

Konak   wooden house in Turkey

Luisa   lemon verbena (*Aloysia citriodora*)

Mabarat   philanthropic society

Mashrabiyya   wooden grillework or lattice placed on windows or used as screens to shield women from view

Mulid al-Nabi   birthday of the prophet Muhammad

Nadi   club

Naskh   an Arabic script

Qirsh   piaster – coin – 1/100 of the Egyptian pound

Qishda   clotted cream

Rakaa   prostration for prayer

Ramadan   Islamic lunar month of fasting

Rihan   basil

Riqaa   an Arabic script characterized by angular letters used also in Ottoman Turkish

Salamlik   male quarters of house used for receiving guests (Turkish)

Sarai   palace or mansion

Shariah   the revealed law of Islam, *Shariah* court is a religious court where personal status or family cases are heard

Shur   cloth envelopes (Turkish), *shurs* made out of silk and embroidered in silver or gold were typical gifts for female guests at marriage ceremonies among the upper class in Huda Shaarawi's time

Sitt al-mistihiyya   literally, 'the shy lady'

Subiyya   barley drink

Suk   market (*Suk al-Asr*: afternoon market)

Tarha   cloth or veil used to cover a woman's hair

Tuffah al-walida   literally, 'mother's apples'

Yali   large, sprawling Turkish house built at the water's edge along the Bosphoros

Zaghruda   sharp, ululating trill women emit on a joyful occasion

Zarf   a round container which holds a tiny, handleless coffee cup, *zarfs* made of precious metals or decorated with precious stones may be reserved for distinguished guests as a mark of special respect

Zifaf   wedding or ceremonials connected with wedding

INDEX

NEW AND FORTHCOMING BOOKS FROM THE FEMINIST PRESS

Anna Teller, a novel by Jo Sinclair. $35.00 cloth, $16.95 paper.

The Captive Imagination: A Casebook on The Yellow Wallpaper,
edited and with an introduction by Catherine Golden.
$35.00 cloth, $14.95 paper.

Fault Lines, a memoir by Meena Alexander. $35.00 cloth,
$14.95 paper.

I Dwell in Possibility, a memoir by Toni McNaron. $35.00 cloth,
$12.95 paper.

Lion Woman's Legacy: An Armenian-American Memoir, by Arlene
Avakian. Afterword by Bettina Aptheker. $35.00 cloth,
$14.95 paper.

*Motherhood by Choice: Pioneers in Women's Health and Family
Planning,* by Perdita Huston. $35.00 cloth, $14.95 paper.

The Princess and the Admiral, by Charlotte Pomerantz, illustrated
by Tony Chen. $17.95 cloth, $8.95 paper.

The Seasons: Death and Transfiguration, a memoir by Jo Sinclair.
$35.00 cloth, $12.95 paper.

Women Writing in India: 600 B.C. to the Present, edited by Susie
Tharu and K. Lalita. Vol. I: 600 B.C. to the Early Twentieth
Century. Vol. II: The Twentieth Century. Each volume $59.95
cloth, $29.95 paper.

For a free catalog, write to The Feminist Press at The City University
of New York, 311 East 94 Street, New York, NY 10128. Send book
orders to The Talman Company, 150 Fifth Avenue, New York, NY
10011. Please include $3.00 postage/handling for one book, $.75 for
each additional book.